AF407158

Things I Learned In The Old School

J.S. Schmidt

OTHER BOOKS BY:

J.S. Schmidt

Learn To Be Still

Roses and Thorns

The Entwining

Remembrance

*Things I Learned in the
Earth School*

THIS BOOK IS DEDICATED TO:

My favorite teachers in the old school: Josephine McCreary, Georgia Lamberson, Dorothy Mason, Lois Brubacher
Also dedicated to the teachers who annoyed me, pushed me, and whose guidance took me many years to come to appreciate. Marjorie Windsor, Helen Stucky, Marie Feland, Gene Ferguson.

Contents

The Journey

Somewhere upon my journey
I met you on the way.
I stopped and watched and listened
To all you had to say.

I took to heart what you gave
I carry it with me now
With all the things I cherish;
You have touched my life somehow.

For all that you have given;
For what you willingly shared;
Please know that I am grateful
For all the ways you cared.

May you always find a blessing
As each day of life you live.
May life grow ever sweeter;
The reward for all you give.

J.S. Schmidt-June 2,2021

Part One

The Old School

Introduction

When I was barely five years old, I was sent to kindergarten. The school was in a beautiful old fashioned limestone building. Twenty years later, it was demolished to be replaced by a one- story red brick structure that in my mind was a pretty sore substitute. The only thing I liked about school was that beautiful old building. It was by far the largest building I had ever been in; everything in it seemed grand. It had two upper stories and a basement or garden level. The lunch room and at least, when I took instrumental music, the band room, were on the lowest level. Going down the stairs to the lunch room always seemed like entering a tunnel. At one end, there was a boiler room that held a boiler that was so large it seemed to nearly fill the entire space.

The upper stories had beautiful polished hard wood floors and ornate tin on the ceilings and down the walls to the wainscoting. The ceilings were very tall and the hallways were very long. There were classrooms on either side of the hallways; when class was in session, it was so quiet you could hear a pin drop; unless someone walked down the hall. The sound of their steps would echo so loudly you could hear it inside the classrooms, even with the doors closed.

Each room had lots of big windows on the outside wall. They let in loads of sunlight and warmth. I have to admit that usually made me drowsy in the afternoons, but thankfully, unlike a few of my classmates, I never actually fell asleep. In the winter, the windows would draw my attention when the snow was falling. I was much more interested in the winter wonderland that was developing outside, than whatever was being presented in class. The windows also reminded me of the fun I could be having at home; they always seemed to trigger daydreams and happy thoughts. Disciplining my mind to think about what my teacher wanted me to think about was a big challenge for me and I resisted it for a long time. I especially resisted learning math. I had no natural curiosity about numbers; words however, filled me with fascination and still do.

At the south end of the first- floor hallway, there hung an old- fashioned clock with a beautiful pendulum. The clock made a very distinctive sound as it ticked away the hours. When we arrived at school in the morning, we were supposed to stand in line under the clock, until the first bell rang. By the time the second bell rang, you were supposed to be in your seat or be counted tardy; being tardy back then was a semi-serious offense. I loved to stand there and watch the clock and listen to the sound of its ticking, but when the bell rang, my heart would sink. We stood under the clock at various other times during the day; after recess and bathroom breaks and after lunch.

My husband is a lover of clocks and we have a lot of them in our home; some rooms have as many as three clocks. We have mantel clocks, kitchen clocks, regulator wall clocks etc.; nearly all of them ring, ding, or chime and none of them agrees with the time on any of the others. Several years ago, the clock from the old school became available at an auction and my husband bought it; he always says that one belongs to me. I still love the sound of it ticking away. It reminds me of the beautiful building I loved, but not the hours I spent there feeling as if I was in captivity. I was sad when the building was demolished; it seemed like a terrible way to reward it for so many years of service to the community.

At the end of each grading period, we were trusted with a report card to deliver safely into the hands of our parents. In the lower grades, the report cards were colorful and there were interesting figures of school children on them, which illustrated each area of study we were being graded on, as well as tasks we were supposed to master. The tasks were things like: plays well with others, listens attentively, follows instructions etc.

In many ways mastering those tasks has turned out to be more important in my life than the more required course of study. These tasks were given a great deal of importance and our teachers made sure we learned them well, in addition to reading, spelling and math. Today, those tasks would likely be referred to as values and many parents would object to them being taught in a public school. In many cases "no one" is teaching these simple, but very important lessons to today's children. Perhaps, there would be more kindness and consideration in the world we live in now, if these things were being taught somewhere by someone. Life can be a struggle and even having a good value system won't always smooth out the bumps, but I hate to think of where I would have been when my life got really rough without these basic rules of conduct to guide me through.

1

Kindness

As I look back at my childhood, it seems that kindness was one of the first concepts I learned. I was encouraged by my parents to be kind to my little sister. They encouraged me to be kind to the girl in our neighborhood who was mean to me. They encouraged me to be kind to the elderly neighbor who falsely accused me of hitting her with my bicycle.

When I went to kindergarten, I realized within the first hour that not everyone had been taught to be kind. When the teacher called each of our names, to check attendance, the little girl in back of me made a derogatory remark about my name and everyone laughed. I began to cry and wanted to go home. The more I cried, the less kind my teacher became. I never told her why I was crying and she never asked me; she assumed I wanted to go home because I missed my mother. In desperation, she threatened to send me to the principal's office, where she informed me, I would be spanked and sent back to class. I had heard some things about the principal from the kids in my neighborhood, and though I had never set eyes on the man, I was terrified of him. So, to recap my first day of kindergarten; I was ridiculed for my strange name, humiliated and threatened; I hated school from that day forward. I spent the rest of my school days seeking to disappear somewhere in the back row of every classroom I entered and rarely doing anything that drew attention to myself. I thought it ironic, even though I didn't actually know the meaning of the word at that time, that my teacher who had been so unkind to me the first day of kindergarten was the person who judged on my report card each grading period, whether or not I was kind.

We lived in a small town and as a whole, it wasn't very diversified; except for a couple of Latino families and a couple of black families, everyone there was white. In my kindergarten class, there was one little black girl, she was very shy and mostly afraid of everyone there; she had been made to repeat kindergarten and was also very self-conscious; the same girl who made fun of my name, tormented her every day. She would steal her crayons so that when the teacher instructed us to get out a certain color, Sandy (not her real name) would start to cry and get in trouble; sometimes the teacher would make her sit outside the door, in the hallway on the "naughty" chair. I felt so bad for Sandy, but I was afraid to try to help her because I didn't want the mean girl to get mad at me and I didn't think the teacher would listen to me. I tried to be as nice to Sandy as I could, but I always felt guilty that I didn't speak up about what was happening to her.

A couple of years later, I was in music class, trying hard to disappear as usual. It was nearing Christmastime and the teacher had us all sitting in a row around the piano, singing Christmas songs. When she wanted us to sing Jingle Bells, she asked a boy named Jimmy, who he would like to have seated in the sleigh next to him. I was horrified when I heard him say my name and everyone began to laugh. I was so humiliated and angry, because I had done absolutely nothing to be singled out in such a way, that I acted very badly and Jimmy ended up with hurt feelings. I got a thorough tongue-lashing from the teacher who told everyone sitting there that she had expected better behavior from me and apparently, I hadn't been taught to be kind and considerate of others feelings. Again, I felt mistreated and misunderstood, but powerless to explain or defend myself from the attack I had done nothing to precipitate.

The teacher was correct, I had been unkind, but I felt like she was to blame for the whole incident; it bothers me to this day that I treated Jimmy badly, but it also bothers me that I didn't feel able to defend myself.

There have been other times in my life, when I was unkind; sometimes I was deliberately unkind. Usually, I felt some justification for my position, but that doesn't change the fact that I hurt someone. In years past, I used what I refer to as my "poison pen" to give someone a very frank piece of my mind. I would say exactly what I was thinking and feeling and it was anything but kind. I have permanently retired my poison pen; I have regrets about those harsh words, spoken in anger. There is a Native American proverb that says: *"The anger of a man becomes a danger to himself, and to others."* When you lose your temper, you lose yourself. I have learned in my spiritual transformation, that it is so important not to let anger manifest itself in your life. Anger is an effort of your ego to control your emotions; in effect, by letting your emotions control you. The things I regret most in my life are the times I was untrue to myself and the times I was deliberately unkind to someone. Even knowing better doesn't always mean we will act better

2

Punctuality

The world I grew up in placed great store on punctuality. Being on time was an expectation nearly everywhere you went; school, church, appointments, performances etc. Being late reflected poorly on you and sometimes, by association, your family as well.

At school, if you were not in your seat by the time the second bell rang, you were considered to be tardy. There was a little box on your report card that recorded the number of times you had been late to school. You were allowed about 3-4 times and then some official action would be taken; that usually meant a phone call to your parents from the principal and detention for you. Staying after school was an extreme hardship for me, because I didn't want to be there in the first place and I certainly didn't want to stay later than everyone else. A call from the principal was personally humiliating for my mother.

We walked to school, but we only lived about 3 blocks away. We were generally able to get there on time, with an occasional exception now and then. Our morning routine at home was pretty unorganized and invariably someone couldn't find their shoes or their homework, or forgot they needed lunch money and Mother couldn't find the checkbook.

Going to church was a lot harder; my father was the minister and the church he served was 40 miles away. Sunday mornings were as chaotic as school days. As children, we resented being rousted out of bed early on a day we didn't have to go to school, so we dragged our feet as much as possible. Someone was nearly always in tears or in trouble as we went out the door.

I always knew it was important to be on time, but still I questioned why it was such a big deal to adults? As I got older, I realized it's mainly a question of respect. It is disrespectful to consistently show up late. These days it seems to be considered less important in a lot of areas. There are few jobs now that require you to punch a time card to prove you arrived on time. People habitually arrive late for appointments and performances.

My husband and I have enjoyed music concerts since the beginning of our time together, but these days we question spending the significant amount of money it requires to attend these events because of the lateness and other disrespectful behavior of many others who also attend.

The town I grew up in was fortunate to have a young band director in the school system; he was there for about twenty years. In that time, he turned our band program into the envy of many in the state. People actually moved to our small town so their children could be taught by him. He had a method of teaching children to play music that was invariably successful. He set high standards and his expectation that the students meet them was paramount to their success. He could be tough and a lot of parents and students didn't appreciate that. One of the things he was stringent about was punctuality: the way he put it was: *"If you aren't 15 minutes early; you're late!"* Any student he ever taught, remembers those words.

Being on time is simply a matter of being respectful to those who will be inconvenienced by your tardiness. Of course, there are times things happen that thwart your best intentions; but everyone knows that doesn't happen often enough to excuse habitual lateness. Keeping to a schedule is an unfortunate necessity in the earth school; but I find it something to look forward to that there is no time in heaven. Over the years, I've learned not to overschedule myself, not to schedule things I really don't want to do, and to leave earlier and allow for whatever contingency might occur that could make me late.

3

Attentiveness

nother measure of our behavior and performance at school, was a little box on our report card next to a phrase that read: Listens attentively. That little box was usually marked with an S in my case, meaning sometimes. As a child, my mind was always active; I was always thinking, but unfortunately, not always about the subject at hand. Even as an adult, I sometimes struggle with being focused on what's going on in the "now" moment.

The reason attentiveness was considered to be a desired quality in the old school; is that it shows mental discipline, as well as respect for the person who is speaking. Not showing this courtesy and respect, was considered nearly as rude as talking over someone who was speaking. The unwritten rule was, don't talk while the teacher is speaking; don't interrupt people while they are talking and give whoever has the floor your undivided attention.

It was never my intention to be disrespectful by letting my mind wander; it just happened and it happened a lot. My mind is always absorbed with creating something and as I've discovered recently, with the inspiration I receive regarding the books I write, often, if you don't acknowledge inspiration when it comes, it disappears and is lost.

In spite of the fact that attentiveness is something I still

14

struggle with, I am acutely aware of its importance in life. To begin with, you lose a lot of important information when you are only half listening. I also agree that not paying attention when people are speaking to you is rude and inconsiderate. Those are two qualities I really don't want to be known for.

I remember how inadequate I felt as a child, when I was trying to tell someone something that very much mattered to me, and they would look past me and focus on someone else; or just look bored and turn and walk away.

In my heart, I want to make people feel important and accepted; the way every human being deserves to feel. I don't want to hurt anyone's feelings by making them feel insignificant. None of us is ever all that we can be, but I put much more focus on being kind, polite, and respectful to other people than I used to and I know I have the old school to thank for planting the value of these things in me, so many years ago. Many of the lessons I learned as a child, took awhile to gel; I sometimes chose to ignore them, but my conscience never failed to remind me of their importance.

In a former book, I wrote about how good I used to feel about being able to multi-task. My son, Jeff, is an electric lineman and he once told me no one should multi-task, because it can be dangerous. Working with electricity can be deadly and you can only give your full attention to one thing at a time. Trying to do more than that can also affect the quality of the work you do, even if it isn't dangerous.

As I have grown spiritually, I have come to realize that attentiveness and mindfulness are very closely related. Both require you to focus squarely on what's happening in the current moment. Mindfulness living, in a spiritual context, helps you find meaning in everything. How many people claim to be searching the world over to find the meaning of life? It is in mindfulness that meaning is to be found. You can look outside yourself for your entire life and never discover what lies inside you. I believe most of us go through life "attentively" focused on all of the wrong things. We have choices when it comes to deciding where to place our attention.

4

Helpfulness

Next to love, faithfulness, loyalty and compassion, help-fulness is one of the most important gifts we have to give. We often need the help of others, though many of us are reluctant to receive it. We like to think of ourselves as being independent and a little independence can be a good thing. The problem with the concept of independence is that it's only a short jump to separateness. One of the definitions of sep-arateness is: "to isolate". On the level of spirit, this is exactly what we should not do. We are all in this together, as spirits; it is our humanness that strives to differentiate. In order to do that, we are required to judge others in some way, based on whatever criteria we have established that sets us apart.

On a human level, we who lived and studied in the old school, we're taught that helping others was part of our responsibility to family, friends, community, state and country; these days I would add a responsibility to the world, as well.

Being unwilling to help someone in need is easily interpreted as coming from a position of selfishness. Selfishness was really frowned upon in the old school.; in fact, it was openly considered a character flaw and steps were often taken to correct it before it could grow into a deep-seated belief of superiority. In Luke 10:

25-37 Jesus tells the story of the good Samaritan; it describes a scene where a person of one ethnicity is called upon by conscience, to come to the aid of a person of another ethnicity that sees him as less worthy of consideration. They have each been taught to shun the other. He not only renders help at the scene of the man's distress, but helps him to a place of safety where he can be cared for, then he leaves money to assure the man gets all he requires to recover. In many instances, Jesus, as well as the master teachers of other religions, implores us to be helpful to those who are in need of assistance. We are also asked to give whatever assistance we can give with a cheerful heart. As we give, we receive, but giving to receive negates any good that comes from the gift.

Helping others can take many forms, it isn't always money or goods that are needed, though many find it easier to give these gifts than to give something of themselves. In most situations a quick evaluation will tell you what is needed; you make the choice to give it or to find someone else who can, if it isn't in your power to do so. I seriously doubt that there have been many situations where someone refused help to one who was in need and walked away feeling good about their actions. In helping someone, you receive a warming in your heart that you can actually feel with your physical senses. This sense of warmth is a good indication that heaven is smiling on you because of the action you took in helping someone in need.

5

Politeness

In the old school, politeness mattered; it mattered a lot. The lack of politeness spoke volumes about who you were. It not only announced to others that you were rude, it said you were inconsiderate, unkind, ungracious and behaved inappropriately. To behave in such a way, not only reflected on your own character, it reflected on your parents and the rest of your family. Who must they be, if they had not taught you better? It showed a lack of respect for others, as well as yourself.

One of the biggest regrets of my life is that I was often rude and disrespectful to my mother during my teenage and young adult years. When I finally grew up, I realized there is never an excuse for rudeness; there is always another avenue open to you. As with so many other behaviors, rudeness is a choice; you can always choose to be otherwise.

Our society seems to be degenerating at a rapid pace; the teachings of the "old school", no longer hold a place of importance for many people. It can't be totally attributed to the fact that the people who were taught there have died or aged out of the flow of society. One possible reason for the demise of manners could be that it requires you to consider the feelings of others before your own.

When I was in high school there was a new science fiction

TV series; Star Trek. I found it not only fascinating but a great way to escape whatever was going on that I didn't want to think about. I guess a lot of other people liked it too; it's been in syndication for over 50 years. One of the main characters was Lt. Commander Spock; a half-human half-Vulcan, whose primary characteristic was logic. He was often conflicted by the inherent differences within himself that his split genetic makeup created. Whatever challenges these differences presented for him could always be resolved by his belief in the fact that *"the needs of the many, outweigh the needs of the few."* In other words, other people need us to behave in a way that is beneficial to all and isn't just indulgent to our own desires as individuals. There is an old saying: *"No man is an island"*, which further states the wrongmindedness of believing individual need outweighs the collective need for us to support and respect each other.

Politeness is just one brick in that wall or just one thread in the fabric of our society, but it is a very important thread and should not be overlooked or discarded. The standards/values that were taught in the old school were aimed at maintaining a level of respect and concern for others that has helped to preserve us as a nation deserving of the respect and admiration of the world. It is no coincidence that we are no longer thought of as "the shining city on the hill". Our foundation seems to be crumbling beneath us and it may be our own lack of recognition of the importance of values such as these, that will be our undoing. We cannot be a great nation, and a world leader, unless we realize our greatness lies in individual and collective honor and respect.

6

Neatness

On that colorful report card, they handed out to us in kindergarten, there was a box to check, next to a statement that read: "Comes to school neat and clean". In today's ultra-casual world, that probably seems like an unnecessary thing to focus on, but in the old school, it was pretty important. Even in the years my own children went to school, most parents made the effort to see that their children were dressed appropriately.

When my sister worked at the elementary school in the town where we formerly lived, I would often pick her up when school was out, so I sat and watched each day as the children came out. I would see children who had been sent to school in clothes that were dirty, or torn. Sometimes I saw children come out dressed in the pajamas they had worn to bed the night before; my sister said they had wet the bed in the pajamas they wore to school.

Before you jump on me about those people who can't afford to dress their children nicely, let me say this: my grandfather and grandmother raised eight children during the Depression years. It was a struggle just to feed a family that large, let alone provide clothing for them. They were never sent to school in dirty clothes. My grandfather was also an ordained minister; his children didn't have nice "church clothes" and neither did the children of most of his church members. He always said that when you went to church you should wear your best, to show respect. He meant that if a clean pair of overalls that were torn, was the best you had, God would appreciate the effort you made to be there and be respectful.

You might be asking yourself: *"What difference does it make?* Or you might be saying: *"It's no one else's business how my children are dressed."* Those are valid thoughts, but there is another way of thinking about this: there's a bigger picture.

It's first of all a lesson in appropriateness. You can't show up for your court date, wearing your pajamas and fuzzy slippers; that's been done, but the judge wasn't happy and it's usually a good idea to try to please the judge. The inappropriateness of this attire shows disrespect for the legal process. It would be no more appropriate for your surgeon to show up in the operating room wearing swim trunks and a snorkel; it certainly wouldn't appear that he was taking your surgery very seriously. These are just extreme examples to make the point I'm trying to convey.

Research has been done that clearly shows a direct correlation between the way we dress and the way be behave, as well as the way we learn and perform tasks. If we are appropriately attired for whatever situation we are in, we take our jobs more seriously and others take us more seriously too. We listen more carefully, follow directions more precisely and this is not to mention the boost in confidence it gives us. While we may not be consciously aware of these things as they happen; our subconscious mind reacts in a consistent manner to how we are feeling about what we do. Dressing appropriately gives us an edge before we even begin and helps ensure our success.

Your next argument might be: *"Well, who's to say what's appropriate and what isn't?"* That's a fair question; the answer is: it changes from one situation to the next However, if you're paying attention, it doesn't take you long to figure it out. Many times, as with school or work- related situations, you are given guidelines to assist you in dressing properly.

At one time, I worked in the office where my husband was employed as the Sales Administrator. A woman we knew who attended our church, worked there also; she was the receptionist for many years. She was always dressed neatly and professionally. When she retired, her position was given to a younger woman who was already working there in another department. At some point, the owner of the company agreed to let the employees observe Casual Fridays. The new receptionist began wearing old ragged jeans and football jerseys, along with her favorite pair of flip-flops.

The receptionist was the first person customers and business associates of the owner saw when they entered the building. The owner was a multi-millionaire and so were most of his business associates; they spent their leisure hours at an exclusive country club. That doesn't make them better than the rest of us, but let's say it elevates their expectations. The woman's attire did not represent the company in a professional or pleasing manner.

Her attire would be completely appropriate for mowing her lawn or running errands, but not as a professional person work-ing in an office setting. Our society has become so enamored with comfort, that we have degenerated into carelessness and thoughtlessness as to how we present ourselves to other people. I love to be comfortable just as much as the next person, but I know it always boosts my level of confidence when I feel I'm well put together. If you want to be sharp; it helps to look sharp. Just saying...

Rev. Roy Pierce and wife Flora, my grandparents, with their eight children.

7

Honesty

There are some very well-known clichés relating to honesty, that we've all heard hundreds of times; *"Honesty is the best policy"; "Just tell the truth"* etc. The dictionary describes honesty as the quality of being fair and truthful. It sounds pretty straightforward, but of all the classic virtues, it may be the hardest to achieve consistently. I believe that's because you have to weigh each situation and the degree of honesty that's appropriate. If you choose to not share complete honesty about something, the appropriateness of that decision depends on your reasons for it. For instance, if you're in a situation where telling the whole, unfiltered truth would hurt someone, and the benefit of complete honesty doesn't justify the pain it would inflict, perhaps perfect honesty isn't the best choice.

If you find yourself in a court of law, being totally honest would be the appropriate choice. But again, we all have our own perspective when it comes to the truth. In the time we are living through now, truth and facts seem to carry little weight. We choose what we believe is true, regardless of fact. Sometimes, we find one version of the truth to be more palatable to us because it more closely coincides with our personal belief system.

Honesty can seem like a hard concept to a child, but perhaps it's even more difficult as we age and life becomes more complex. I'm not advocating dishonesty, just that there are degrees of appropriate honesty.

We are all familiar with the "little white lie". I would say a white lie could be categorized as a "harmless" lie; others might say a white lie could start you down the slippery slope to telling bigger, more harmful lies.

The problem with lies is that it's harder to remember something that isn't true, than it is to just tell the truth. If you tell multiple lies to multiple people, you really have a lot of untruths to try to recall, as well as, which lies you told to which person. Your life becomes more complicated with each lie you tell. There is another old saying about honesty; *"truth will out"*, which means: the truth will always reveal itself; it may take time, but truth will emerge.

When I was younger, I assumed people told lies deliberately to deceive you; that isn't always the case. Often, people don't tell you the truth because they don't want to hurt you. When I realized my first marriage was one big lie, I believed that every lie I was told was deliberate and malicious; now I know it was much more complicated than that.

As a child, I was taught to be honest at home, at school and at church.; the community I grew up in placed a high value on honesty. Yet, as an adolescent, I fell into telling "convenient" lies pretty easily. I always struggled with the truth, if I thought it would hurt someone's feelings. As an adult, I try to tell the truth as gently as I can; that's not always possible. I try to never tell a lie at all, but especially not in a malicious context.

Spiritually, I believe we are all in this together and it's vital that we are all able to trust each other, because love is dependent on trust. There are just as many ways to tell the truth as there are to be dishonest, but in being truthful, we can choose words that are kind and gentle, because words are powerful. They can wound or they can heal; they can hurt or they can comfort. Brutal honesty isn't a positive thing; it's a weapon.

8

Fairness

The concept of fairness can be a bit tricky because we each have our own sense of what we perceive as being fair. This is why the concept of judges needing to be impartial came into being. It is why there are mediators and negotiators. Often however, it isn't possible to find a solution that is fair to everyone. The story in the Bible about two mothers who both claimed that the same child was theirs, Illustrates this point well. The two women lived in the same household and each cared for an infant of the same age. One of the babies died and each claimed the surviving child as their own. King Solomon was in the unenviable position of determining who would get the child. When neither of them would admit the child was not hers, he suggested cutting the child in half, with each one receiving half of what would then be a deceased baby. One of the mothers was content with his ruling; the other pleaded with him to give the child, alive and well to the other claimant. In doing so, she revealed herself to be the actual mother of the child and the other woman to be the fraud. Her willingness to give up her child in order to save it revealed the depth of her love.

We've all heard the saying, *"life isn't fair"*, and at some point that statement will apply to each of us; we'll all *"win some and lose some"*. How we handle these events that we deem "unfair", can seriously effect the course of our lives. It is difficult for us to accept a decision that doesn't go our way, if we feel the cards were deliberately stacked against us. We feel we were treated badly and most of us carry around feelings of resentment, that we believe we are entitled to have. Resentment, otherwise known as "baggage", is damaging to your spirit and if you allow enough baggage to accumulate, it will weigh you down and effect your relationships with everyone else.

I used to carry a lot of baggage; I knew I had the option of discarding it, but I chose not to. That would have required a whole lot of forgiveness and I wasn't good at that. It wasn't until I forgave the unforgivable, the murder of my son, that I finally realized carrying resentment doesn't hurt anyone but the person who's lugging it around.

As a matter of fact, I continue to consider it supremely unfair that someone took my son's life. That act was critically unfair to so many people, and unfortunately, some of them are carrying a huge load of anger and resentment because of it. I was able to make the choice to forgive the act, though not without help from heaven; I couldn't have done it alone. I will always believe it was unfair that someone took Ethan from his family; but I carry no anger or resentment about it. I carry the pain of loss and the longing to see my son, but I know with the deepest conviction that I will see my son and be with him in another place, when the time is right.

Sometimes, we simply have to accept that life isn't fair. It is undeniably true that we experience the most profound spiritual growth through adversity. In a perfect world that wouldn't be necessary; this world is far less than perfect. I believe we will all reach a perfect place of existence; but it will take some of us much longer to get there. Life here will continue to be unfair because human beings make it so. We have the choice to create fairness in this world, but it is a choice many fail to consider.

In the "old school", we frequently would hear *people say: "it isn't whether you win or lose, it's how you play the game."* In today's world, people seem to want to win no matter the cost. The "cost" isn't always a monetary loss; it's often a loss of personal integrity, as well as reputation. When you lose your integrity; you haven't been true to your authentic self; so even if you win, you still lose.

One of the things that most often causes people to not play "fair" is money. When we introduce money into a situation, attitudes begin to change rapidly. Fairness is no longer the main concern. In our society today, money equals success and success is seen as the ultimate win. Our children are learning that being successful is about earning money. No one tells them that money and success won't always make for a happy life. People who win huge lottery jackpots frequently report that their "good luck" cost them everything that mattered to them.

Many people expect life to treat them fairly, but don't see anything wrong with their own unfair treatment of others. It is universally true that you get back what you give out, so if you want to be treated fairly the only chance of that happening is to do the same to others. You manifest for yourself what you create with your words and actions.

9

Humility

*H*umility seems to be hard to define; it is easier to say what it is not. If you are humble, you are not arrogant, haughty or proud. The use of the word proud has changed since I was a child. If people said you were proud, back then, it usually meant you were "full of yourself". In those days, that wasn't considered a positive thing. The Bible says we are to be humble, like Jesus. Proverbs 16:18 says, *Pride goeth before destruction, and a haughty spirit before a fall."*

It is easy to confuse pride with confidence; having confidence in yourself and your abilities isn't a negative thing. Confidence or faith in yourself is a necessary part of having the courage it takes to live in the world. There's nothing inherently bad about pride. Most of us are proud of things we have worked diligently to accomplish; we're proud of our families etc. It is only when pride pushes us to believe we are superior to others, that it shifts into a negative stance. Pride of this kind leads us to be boastful and haughty.

In our success driven society today, humility is seen as weakness, and I'll admit it's hard to be driven and humble at the same time. We've probably all known someone who would have us believe they've been everywhere and seen everything; someone who talks about themselves incessantly. While most of us find that annoying, the real problem with it is that if you believe you know everything, you can't be taught anything. Life is meant to teach us and in learning we grow. In life's greatest trials we learn who we are spiritually and spirit is what drives our actions as human beings.

I remember how important it seemed in my early years at school to be the first one to get to do something, anything. If you got to be the first one in line for lunch or recess, your position was envied by nearly everyone. I was rarely ever first because a lot of teachers do everything alphabetically and my last name was Pierce, so no matter which end of the alphabet they started from, I was somewhere in the middle. In many ways, I was fine with that, because I was really just trying to blend in with whatever group I happened to be in. The less notice I received the better I liked it. I wasn't being humble; I was just shy and had low self-esteem.

If you are truly humble, you realize that no matter how successful you are at anything, you didn't rise to the top all by yourself. If you are spiritually humble, you realize whatever success you achieve in this life is temporary and won't get you a place above anyone else in the next life. No matter how high you fly in this life, at some point, the wind will shift and you'll be brought down to a lower level. You may rise and fall many times during your human life and there is a lesson to be learned each time life takes you to the heights and also when it allows your progress to recede. Perhaps, the greatest lesson in all of this is that things will always change and that we shouldn't become accustomed to being first or best, because we will all take our turn at failure. When our turn comes to be in a lower place, we must learn not to let our emotions sink too low; just as we should not let our emotions become too exalted when we have our turn at the top of the world. If we are well grounded and humble in spirit, we can live harmoniously in either sphere.

I have learned many things through the worst times of my life and one of the most important of these is to let life come to me, instead of trying to make it what I think it should be. What comes of it's own is almost always better than anything I could have imagined.

10

Responsibility

When I was around 10 years old and wanted to be able to do more things apart from my family, my mother told me; *"with greater privilege, comes greater responsibility"*. There are so many ways to demonstrate responsibility, but it basically just means to be accountable. Initially in my case, that meant being responsible enough to follow the rules about where I went, who I was with, and to come home at the designated time. In this regard, I couldn't have been deemed to be a very responsible person. In other ways, such as helping at home, I walked a straighter line. Just before I entered high school, my mother went to work in a nearby town; it became my responsibility to prepare an evening meal for my family, every day. When I began to officially date, I had to prepare a meal for my family even if I was going out to eat. I was also responsible for the grocery buying, as well as the cleaning.

I always struggled with taking responsibility for my mistakes; I was pretty good at making excuses or blaming someone else. I always knew when I was wrong; I just never wanted to admit it; I know a lot of other people who have the same problem. Of course, I grew up some and got better at accepting my part in whatever had gone wrong, but in some instances, I still struggled. I don't think it was that I thought other people would be disappointed in me, it was that I would feel disappointed in myself. I had very low self-esteem when I was young and my mistakes seemed to confirm my already low opinion of myself.

There is the concept of personal responsibility, but there is also the concept of responsibility to others and the concept of responsibility **for** others. Being responsible to yourself is probably not a virtue, because that comes pretty naturally, but taking responsibility for others is a choice we make. It is a self-less act; a noble act that not everyone sees the need for.

There is something called the "collective consciousness", which is defined as "the totality of beliefs and sentiments common to the average citizens of the same society." Our judicial code, the laws we have passed to govern our conduct, are part of the collective consciousness. In general, we all agree that we will obey the law; it is our responsibility to each other. We all agree that we will not betray our country, or steal our neighbor's car, etc.

When the collective consciousness begins to break down, as it has in recent years, society as a whole suffers. Likewise, when you consistently act in a manner that is untrue to yourself and your concept of who you are, you damage your own consciousness, as well as the collective consciousness.

When people feel they have no responsibility for the welfare of others, they fail to teach their children to be responsible also. In order to maintain an orderly society, we can't all come to the place where we only recognize responsibility to ourselves and our individual needs and desires. We all teach by example and our actions, as well as our attitudes speak volumes to others, especially the young.

Being responsible, begins with ourselves, but it definitely doesn't end there; it is like ripples on a pond. We are not born with a sense of responsibility; it must be consciously instilled in each individual person. In the "old school", it was considered paramount to growing "good people", who would become good citizens of the world.

11

Respect

Respect... now that is a deep subject, indeed. Respect used to be taught and expected almost everywhere. It was something you earned; no one owed it to you. Today, people believe they're born with a right to it, and while I'll agree that every human being deserves to have their dignity respected, that's not exactly the type of respect I'm referring to here.

One example that comes to mind, would be an old attitude that all children were taught; "respect your elders". In today's world older people are very often not respected. They are not appreciated for the life they've lived, or the contributions they have made, or the sacrifices they have made for their families, society, and their country. In the past, people looked to their elders for guidance in the most important aspects of life: such as, faith, marriage and child rearing.

A few years ago, I was with my sister and overheard a conversation she had with a woman who was some years younger than we were, but old enough to have just become a grandmother for the first time. Her son and his wife told her their pediatrician had issued this piece of advice: *"Don't listen to your parents, they don't know anything about children."* I was astonished! When I was a very young mother, the best advice

I got, came not from my doctor, but from older mothers and grandmothers. Another concept you learned in the old school is that *"experience is the best teacher."* Job 12:12 says: *"is not wisdom found among the aged? Does not long- life bring understanding?"*

There are many different sides to the concept of respect. There is personal respect, professional respect, relational respect, self-respect; and there are many different schools of thought regarding each.

In general thought, this is a good time to bring in the Golden Rule: *"Do unto others as you would have them do to you."* In other words, treat people the way you want them to treat you. We were taught this concept at home, at school and in church; it doesn't seem to be taught much of anywhere now. It is the concept at the heart of respect; give to others the respect you wish for yourself.

One of the things that I always found to be of concern, was the lack of simple respect most children are shown by adults, often including their parents. Many people scream and curse at their young children in public to such a degree that it makes you wonder how much worse these children could be treated at home, when no one is there to observe what happens. We all lose our temper occasionally out of frustration or stress, but it should never become a habit to speak to a child in such a way. I and so many like me who have suffered the loss of a precious child, am appalled that anyone would abuse their child. Anytime I felt a pang of conscience regarding something I said to one of my children or if I felt I treated them unfairly etc., I apologized. It benefits children immensely to know that parents are human beings and no more perfect than they are.

I believe the most important kinds of respect are self-respect and respect of others as human beings/spirits. Many people seek the highest degrees of professional respect; that doesn't make you anymore worthy of personal respect than you already are as a human being and it won't necessarily make you more likely to respect other people. Only when we come to view all human beings as equal in the sight of God, or whatever name you feel comfortable with for the Source of All Life; can we learn respect without judgement.

In my own mind, I feel the most serious lack of respect shown today, is lack of respect for human life. How has the concept of human life become so much less sacred? Perhaps, it's reflective of the fact that everything in our lives has become less sacred. The loss of respect for life is the ultimate measure of how far we have fallen as a society. Life should be held as the most precious thing we have; without human life we have nothing here, everything in this world is meaningless. Life is the indescribably beautiful gift we all receive from God. How inconceivably sad that the magnificence of this gift should be diminished by disrespect and pure thoughtlessness.

12

Courtesy

s I mentioned previously, being courteous was something you were graded on at the old school. It was an
expectation that you would treat others courteously. The definition of courteousness is: marked by respect for and consideration
of others. Back then, being impolite or disrespectful was likely
to get the same reaction as slapping someone across the face.

In the past there were a lot of socially acceptable ways to
show courtesy to other people. Today, people find this kind of
consideration of others ridiculous, or at the least, quaint and
unnecessary. Here are a few examples of old-fashioned courteousness: if you met someone on the sidewalk and there wasn't
room for you to pass side by side, out of courtesy, one would
step aside while the other passed. If one of these persons was a
male, it was proper for him to step aside and let a female pass. If
you were seated in a room with limited capacity and an elderly or
disabled person entered and found no seat available, it would be
considered courteous behavior for you to offer your seat to them.

We were taught everywhere we went, at school,
at church or any other public place, to say please,
thank you and you're welcome, whenever called for.

My husband and I love to go to music concerts; we pay

for good seats and we arrive early. We are often disheartened at the rudeness of others who attend these events. They are rude to each other, to the ushers and to the performers. Many times, they talk loudly during the performance or yell offensive things to the performers. If at a venue that serves alcohol, they leave their seats many times to refill their drinks, which means they disturb everyone in the row they are seated in, while they get in or out. If you were to complain about this behavior, you would be the one considered out of line.

Being courteous, costs you absolutely nothing. Like so many other things in life, it is a choice you make; sadly today, many people don't even consider it as an option. Courtesy is closely tied to so many other concepts taught in the old school, such as; kindness, respect, dignity, selflessness etc. Courtesy says a lot about you; your lack of it speaks volumes and everything it says is negative.

The biggest question today is this: if the old school doesn't exist anymore, if the majority of people don't have any affiliation with church or mindfulness philosophies, if parents are too busy or don't see the necessity; where will people learn the importance of developing such traits as courtesy? The way we treat each other as human beings and fellow spirits, is of extreme importance if you are capable of seeing the" big picture". A disappointingly large number of people, never consider the "big picture".

13

Consideration

Going back to my early years in school, our report card in the younger grades included a box to mark, with a notation beside it that read: "is considerate". The definition of consideration is: "kindness and thoughtful regard for others, or an act of thoughtfulness." Once we got up to the higher grades, none of the boxes such as the one regarding consideration appeared on our report card. I guess they must have figured by that time, the concept had been presented often enough and the lesson had been learned. As I look back at those years and my own behavior, as well as the behavior of some of my classmates, I can see the lesson was not as well taught as it was assumed to be.

When I observe what is acceptable behavior of human beings toward each other today, I wonder if anyone really retained the concept of consideration? It is a rare thing to see. Perhaps, the illustration of the concept of thoughtfulness and consideration, would be my own husband. He has always been very considerate of me and others he cares deeply for. He rarely makes a move without first considering what it would mean for me. He does very thoughtful things for me on special occasions, but he often does those things quite out of the blue.

Humans are not born with values such as consideration.

We are born self-absorbed, and in many instances, impatient and insistent that our needs should be met sooner rather than later. Values must be learned and in order for that to occur, they must be taught. The big question is: Who will teach them?

About the time Ethan graduated from high school, a school board member who belonged to a rather assertive local church, proposed that the school district adopt a value- based educational system. I don't know what his actual motives were, but it certainly raised a ruckus in our little town. Numerous parents appeared at subsequent board meetings to object to "church" being taught in the public school system. Others claimed it was their sacred right as parents to decide what values their children were taught. I'm not disavowing either of those positions, but the question remains: *Who will teach today's children values?*

Statistics show that fewer people than ever before prefer to affiliate themselves with established church organizations. That means it's unlikely their children attend a Sunday School or church school, instead of public institutions. Sometimes, vacation bible school attracts children who don't attend a church; it's usually thought to be more fun and games than Sunday School.

Many children attend a daycare or pre-school, values are rarely taught in those settings either. While it's true that some parents make the effort to teach values in their own home, most don't seem to think it important for their children to learn them. Many parents have little time at home with their children because of work related obligations, and their own, as well as their children's extra-curricular activities.

Many places still offer things like Boy and Girl Scouts or 4-H programs that offer some value-based activities; volunteerism and community service, at the least.

You may be asking yourself why it matters if values aren't being taught? You may assume that children will pick these things up as a natural course, without any formal presentation of them. It matters because we now live in a society filled with rudeness, unkindness, selfishness, violence and even our schools are breeding grounds for brutish bullies. This, in spite of the number of school districts that pat themselves on the back while touting their "zero tolerance policies", that supposedly address that issue successfully. As children mature into adults, it matters so much more what kind of person and citizen they will become. What grade they received in math or science may be important, but not nearly as important as how they treat their fellow human beings. It matters most of all who they are and what they will teach their own children. The future of our world depends on the values we teach and live by.

My fourth grade class; I am the girl in the center of the front row. Miss Lamberson is standing on the right side, in the second row. She was very calm, kind and respectful in her treatment of students she taught.

14

Self-Discipline

It seems odd to me that so many things we teach our children are aimed at helping them develop self-control and yet there are so many adults today who seem to have none. Even if children are raised by parents who fail to teach these concepts, they are taught at daycare, at school, at church, etc.

I realize life isn't like it was in the old school, now considered "the dark ages", but without some degree of inner discipline how is it possible to come together in any regard and accomplish something. If we all talk at once and no one listens, how can we make decisions? If we spend all of our time arguing over who deserves to be first, we are essentially paralyzed; we can't move forward. If we say everything we are thinking to everyone, in every situation, people get hurt, people get angry and want to separate themselves from the group. If we don't discipline ourselves to follow traffic rules, accidents happen and people get hurt; sometimes people die. These are only a few examples of the damage we can do without self-discipline.

Society seems to believe today, that any kind of restraint or restriction is an infringement on personal freedom. Any action, no matter what they choose to do, is an expression of their free will and therefore should be considered appropriate.

Back in the "good old days", you weren't allowed to do things that carelessly or deliberately hurt other people. There was an expectation that you understood that and would act accordingly. If not, you could expect that there would be consequences for your actions. Today many people reject expectations and consequences. I am appalled that people think it's okay to threaten the life of someone you disagree with politically, or in any other circumstance. The fact that these threats are often documented on social media and there are no consequences completely astonishes me. Personal threats of bodily harm or death are against the law in this country, yet there don't seem to be repercussions unless actual harm comes to someone. That is like "closing the barn door after the horse runs away"; in other words, it's too late to be of any value to the one threatened.

In spite of the efforts of many parents, grandparents, teachers and clergy, to teach children to be kind, considerate, and to control their impulses, we see adults who are totally out of control and much of their bad behavior is deliberate. What hope do the children of these people have of learning to function in an "appropriate way?" An appropriate way in this context often pertains to your safety and mine.

Before someone starts shouting about parent shaming, let me acknowledge it isn't only parents who are responsible for this epidemic of bad and unacceptable behavior; television networks, Hollywood and the recording industry and social media do more than their fair share.

On the dedication page of this book, you will find a list of the names of some of my former teachers; some I remember fondly and some I remember as antagonists. The number one name on the list of antagonists should be Mr. Ferguson; he was the Jr. High Science teacher and football coach. Mr. Ferguson and I rarely saw things the same way. He was tough and I had a real lack of self-discipline. He was very determined to change that and he made my life miserable for the entire time I was in 7th and 8th grade. It was a battle royal from beginning to end. He set a standard for me that was a lot higher than anyone else in the class, because he believed I had the capacity to do that much better.

Many years after I graduated from high school and he had retired from teaching, I inadvertently ran into him in the public library in my hometown. I wasn't planning to speak to him, but he was having none of that; he spoke first and he said: *"Well, Miss Pierce, you still hate my guts, don't you!"* I was caught completely off-guard and the only thing I could think of to say was: *"I wouldn't say that."*

By the time we had this chance meeting, I was aware that he had only been trying to help me; the problem was I didn't want his help and didn't appreciate his methods. I've never understood how anyone reacts positively to negative messaging. I know his intentions were good and I understand now how important self-discipline is. I give him credit for trying.

It isn't hard to understand why children who have never been taught self-discipline might grow up to be undisciplined adults. It's harder to understand how children who have been reared with concepts such as self-discipline and kindness etc. grow up to become undisciplined adults. The answers must lie in outside influences, lack of self-esteem or outright emotional rebellion. I have to ask myself, why are so many of today's children so angry?

You might be asking yourself why any of this bears examination? The answer as I see it is this: It matters first in family relationships and expands all the way to global relationships. We must find a way to live in peace and harmony before we destroy all we have been given. That requires mutual respect and restraint in our attitudes and behaviors toward each other. I still believe we can make this world a better place, which will allow us more time and space to focus on why we are here and what comes next for each of us.

Mr. Ferguson, standing on left, back row,
basketball team with cheerleaders.

15

Patience

🍎🍎🍎🍎🍎🍎🍎🍎🍎🍎🍎🍎🍎🍎🍎🍎🍎🍎🍎🍎🍎

During the years I was raising my children, I often told them: *"Life requires patience."* As infants we are completely self-absorbed and quite demanding. We want what we need immediately; if we have loving, attentive parents our needs are quickly met. It isn't long, however, before we have to learn that we will sometimes have to wait for what we want or need. As we grow older, we may have to wait for longer and longer periods of time to have our needs attended to, as perhaps, someone with a more urgent need is looked to first.

Our society puts great store in being first. Is it any wonder there is so little patience to be found in the world? We must be taught to be patient and often that requires us to place the needs of others before our own. We are many times offended when someone else's needs are judged to be greater than ours.

In Matthew 20:16 Jesus said: *"So the last will be first, and the first last. For many are called, but few are chosen."* It was His way of telling us the world is topsy-turvy; in a spiritual sense, we've got it all wrong. There is no honor in being first; it is a useless distinction. In God's eyes we are all the same; our needs are equally important. In spite of that we are often called to wait for what we desire so, impatiently. Obviously, waiting is an important concept or God wouldn't have us do it so often. Proverbs 15:18 says: *"Hot tempers cause arguments, but patience brings peace."* Romans 12:12 says: *"Rejoice in hope, be patient in tribulation, be constant in prayer."* Romans 8:25 says: *"But if we hope for what we do not see, we wait for it with patience."* Colossians 3:12 says: *"Therefore, as God's chosen people, holy and dearly loved, clothe yourselves with compassion, kindness, humility, gentleness, and patience."* Ephesians 4:12 says: *"Be completely humble and gentle; be patient, bearing with one another in love."* This scripture from Ephesians points out that patience is a part of loving others. Jesus calls us to love one another and being patient is a way for us to show our love.

I never knew exactly how much patience life would require, until Ethan's life was taken. There were many days as I reluctantly dragged myself out of bed, that I asked God: *"How long will I have to live without my son?"* God's answer was: *"Be patient."* There were days that I wished I was farther along in my process of grief, so it wouldn't hurt so much. God's answer was: *"Be patient."* There were days I wished I had a place to go to get away from myself and my anguish. God's answer was: *"Be patient."*

Most of my life I was pretty good at getting out of things I found unpleasant, but grief, I discovered, must be addressed. If it isn't addressed, it never gets better. Even when you tell yourself you've hidden it so well no one will know it's there, it will continue to reveal itself in your life, in your dreams, in your responses and your relationships. Grief requires more patience than I ever believed I had. Grief is torturous, but it isn't a punishment; it is the process by which healing comes to us. It is the relief for our sadness and pain, but to receive the heart of that gift, which is peace, we must learn to be patient.

God isn't always going to give us what we want, even if we wait for it. He will always give us what is best, even if we don't understand it.

16

Loyalty

As a young person, I considered loyalty to be a very black or white concept; either you are loyal or you or not. As my life has unfolded, I realize that few things are as simple as that. Loyalty is something that can have many variations, nuances and definitions. It can also be misused, manipulated and misunderstood; so, you see it is anything but simple.

I always considered myself to be fiercely loyal to those I cared about; as I look back, I see that this is also not 100% accurate. Loyalty can be a very short-lived concept; for instance, when two people marry, they vow to be loving and loyal to each other. When a divorce occurs all of the vows are considered to be null and void and loyalty is no longer required.

Loyalty to your friends often changes as you move on to relationships with other people. I guess you could say human beings are loyal until they aren't; if this is true, then what value is there to loyalty to begin with?

I know that as a child who was the product of the "old school", I learned that loyalty meant that you could be counted on to maintain certain attitudes. Some of these attitudes were expected of you and others you chose to uphold on your own.

I was a teenager during the Vietnam war years. My male

classmates were required to register for the draft, which was still in effect at that time. If they refused to do so, they were deemed to be disloyal to their country and could be incarcerated. Women were not required to register or serve in the armed forces. Looking back that somehow seems unfair, but that was the standard then.

I never swore my loyalty to my friends, but I expected they would be loyal to me and I would return that loyalty to each of them. I wouldn't gossip about them or tell any personal secrets they had trusted me with, I wouldn't flirt with their boyfriends etc. I managed to do all of that pretty faithfully until about a year after I got married and learned my husband had betrayed my trust at every turn. My impressions of the value of loyalty and trust became suddenly very jaded. I was wounded to the core and I found it hard to trust anyone; I also decided not to assume anyone was really loyal and not to offer my loyalty to others. This led me into one of the darkest and most difficult periods of my life.

It was only when I met and married my husband Tom, that I learned to trust again. Loyalty is based on trust, respect and faith. It is a crucial part of a positive relationship; any kind of relationship. Loyalty is a pact between two people, each must be dedicated to its protection and preservation and when one of them fails to do that, trust is instantly destroyed. We are loyal to that which we treasure; it requires love, allegiance, faithfulness and often sacrifice for the good of others; it is perhaps the noblest of virtues.

17

Generosity

*M*any people think generosity is about money; that is only partially true. There are many reasons people donate to things, that have nothing to do with a spirit of generosity. For instance, they might do it in order to get a deduction on their taxes, or perhaps, to gain favor with someone who can do something for them in return.

A generous spirit gives more than money; we can give support, strength, perspective, labor and love. I ran across a quote recently; it's attributed to Buddha: *"The greatest gift you can give someone is your time, because when you give your time, you are giving a portion of your life you will never get back."* I was raised with a bit of scripture that was repeated many times in many places and different situations, *"It is more blessed to give than to receive."* Acts 20:35. Jesus also said to give more than what has been asked of you or than is expected.

A generous spirit is a reflection of a happy spirit, a compassionate spirit. I very much want to be remembered as a generous person, not only as it pertains to money. Giving money is perhaps, the least important thing we have to share with others. For many of us, it is easier to give money than to give of ourselves. Not only did Jesus tell us to give, but to give cheerfully and with no expectation of getting something in return. The warm feeling you get from helping someone is the real reward.

We are also not to continue to feel ownership of that which we have given; because as soon as it is received, it no longer belongs to us. I've heard plenty of people say, *"Well, if I'd known they were going to do that with it, I would never have given it to them in the first place."* Think of where we would all be if that was God's attitude about giving. For many people who give, a simple thank you from the receiver is not sufficient to satisfy us that what we gave was appreciated; we expect streamers and balloons!

Giving is its own reward; when we give, we simultaneously receive. I believe the one question that we will be required to answer in heaven is, *"How did you treat others?"* God is love, heaven is about love and generosity is a true measure of your love.

18

Integrity

"A person with integrity acts with honesty,
honor and truthfulness."
-Balance Careers Website

*I*ntegrity is a complex virtue; by that I mean it has multiple singular virtues from which it develops. As children, we were taught to be honest; that meant don't tell lies, don't take things that belong to others, and admit it if you do. Honesty is another important virtue that seems to have become devalued in our society today. Honesty and truthfulness are bound hand in hand; honesty is also bound with fairness; for instance, an honest business person employs fairness in his or her actions with customers and with employees and doesn't mislead anyone about the quality of the products or services of the company he or she owns.

Being honest isn't a part time job; if you are truly honest, you make it your fulltime practice. Being 100% honest is about as hard as being 100% perfect; that's not possible for human beings, but if you strive always to be honest and regret seriously those rare instances when you aren't, you can reasonably be considered an honest person.

Truthfulness is another crucial element of integrity. I believe it is always better to be truthful, unless in doing so, someone else will be hurt. In that case, saying nothing may be best. When it's not possible to remain silent, you should tell the truth as gently and kindly as you can. It is never honorable to feed or to enjoy someone else's humiliation or pain.

Honor is the third component of integrity and perhaps it is a bit harder to define. This isn't the kind of honor that's bestowed on you for achievement, this is personal honor. It is the respect you have for yourself. Without self-respect, integrity can't be achieved or maintained. Self-respect and self-esteem are also bound together and produce the person who behaves honorably, honestly, and truthfully; a person of integrity.

19

Appropriateness

As with many of the topics this book touches on, appropriateness is a complicated subject; it's hard to know where to begin. The subject is only complicated because it attaches itself to so many aspects of behavior. In recent years, I've begun to wonder if they should just remove the word appropriate from the dictionary, because it seems to be so irrelevant in today's thinking.

Appropriateness is so much more than what you wear in a given situation, or using the right fork at a formal dinner; the Oxford Languages says: appropriateness is the quality of being suitable or proper in the circumstance. That's pretty straightforward, while at the same time, it's pretty broad. There are untold numbers of circumstances and it would be impossible to know what is appropriate in all of them.

Many people say, *why bother, just be yourself and that's good enough!* When in doubt, that's probably good advice, but many people know when something is inappropriate and choose to do it anyway; they just don't care. It's a deliberate thumbing of the nose at convention. The idea being that in today's world, convention is just an old-fashioned way of viewing things. The word convention can be a direct substitution for the word custom. Customs are old because they usually develop over a long period of time; but is it wise to discard something that may have value, just because it isn't new? Another word that could be substituted here is tradition; a tradition may be old but it is tradition that seems to give many of us a sense of grounding, of belonging, of being linked to our ancestors. Why should ancestors matter to us today? Because they came to the earth school just as we did; to learn. If we aren't wise enough to look at the past for what has already been learned, it is unlikely we will progress much in our short time here, especially in spiritual growth. On a societal level, disregarding the advancements in social and civil behaviors that were laid down by those of the past, may mean that we will not progress, but regress in our behaviors as human beings. That translates to more violence and disregard for the happiness and safety of all. Once we begin the fall, where does it end? Will we go back to being able to communicate only with grunts and signs, will we truly be living in a world where only the strongest survive, with no consideration of the weak or the sick. What about the elderly? Will they be cast out of the collective because we will no longer see them as having use? Will we look upon those who disagree with us or don't share our physical characteristics, as having no right to live?

Newness is an untested commodity; it has no past by which to be evaluated. We can't see into the future and that which may seem to be so much better than what is old, may turn out to be disastrous. Newness is like a stranger; how do we know if we can trust our safety to it? As with scientific progress, sometimes things that can be done, shouldn't be done; for the good of all.

I'm not saying there isn't value in new things or philosophies or technologies, I'm only saying they should be accepted with caution. Many times, change occurs simply because it's someone's job to make changes. Changes that do not have benefit above and beyond that which already exists, should be questioned and possibly discarded. Just my own opinion.

Whether you are talking about a meeting of the general assembly of the United Nations or a local PTA meeting, there have to be certain things that are agreed upon in order to function and avoid the kind of conflict that prevents the body to function in order to accomplish the group's purpose. The unwritten rules of appropriateness were created for that very purpose; so we can all live together. Even cavemen had rules and if you couldn't live by them, you were cast out of the group to try to make it on your own; that meant you were not likely to survive.

Many of the things I was taught as a child had to do with appropriate behavior. They were things like how to behave in public places. If I acted badly in a store or restaurant, I knew I wouldn't get to go there again until I demonstrated that I knew the rules of behavior. I was taught to whisper in church if I needed to speak during the service. I soon learned it was inappropriate to talk when my teachers were speaking to the class. I learned to be kind and not hurt someone's feelings. I learned I couldn't always be first. I learned not to be upset or angry if I wasn't the winner every time I played a game. I learned to share. I learned not to call people names, or laugh at their expense. I learned to be truthful, without being hurtful to someone else. I learned to follow the rules and why it was important.

People are so confused about many things these days; the world seems to be one big pot of chaos. Even people who want to do the right thing, often don't know what that would entail. I haven't always appreciated rules or been able to follow them perfectly, but I see the need to have them and it concerns me that so many people are blind to the shredding of the fabric of our society. We are deeply divided at this moment in time and we must find our way back to a place of civility and cooperation. Until recently, I just couldn't understand how our country could have come to the point of Civil War in the 1860's, now we hear words like revolution and coup carelessly thrown about by those who are disgruntled

for whatever reason or cause they espouse. Finding common purpose won't be easy, but it is the appropriate course of action in a
democracy and in my own mind, the alternative is unacceptable.

20

Graciousness

raciousness, like humility, is hard to define; we know it when we see it, but we struggle to put it into words. When I look at the way various dictionaries define graciousness, I see definitions that fit life in today's world, but I was pleased to find one that closely fits the one I was taught in my childhood: "graciousness is the quality or state of being benevolent, courteous and kind." So, in essence, graciousness is several virtues combined; there are chapters in this book relating to each of these three virtues. Graciousness itself, isn't nearly as often seen as each of the three independent virtues that comprise it; it is quite rare. It is rare because it isn't often that we combine these three virtues in one act. It is possible to combine any number of virtues, in our interactions with others, but this combination creates something unique. Its uniqueness is related to the fact that it is so seldom observed in today's world. People are often not kind, or generous, or courteous.

I remember years ago, former President George H. Bush, in his inaugural address to the nation, calling for a "kinder, gentler America." Sadly, that didn't happen in his lifetime. We are much less kind today than in 1989, when his presidency began, and that shows no sign of reversing itself.

I consider myself to have a generous spirit and I sincerely hope those who know me well would agree with that assessment. I harbor negative feelings toward stinginess in any form. I try to be a kind person; I say that I try, because I do not always succeed at being so. If I allow myself to become really angry, I can be very unkind. Many people say things in anger that they later claim not to represent their true feelings. As for myself, I know that when I am angry, I am much more likely to say exactly what I feel, because the usual filters of kindness and generosity of spirit are blocked by my anger. One of the most significant ways tragedy has changed me, is that I do not become angry in the same way I used to. Until recently, I wasn't sure I was still able to become angry; I thought perhaps, it just wasn't in me anymore. When given the opportunity to choose whether or not I will let anger take me over, I invariably choose not to give in to it, so as not to relinquish the balance and peace that helps me make it through even the toughest days. Anger requires a lot of energy and I choose to preserve mine for better things.

Sometimes we as human beings, are very reactive and those are the times that anger can strike without warning and with no opportunity to choose otherwise. I won't relate the incident that occurred recently, that showed me this is so. I was suddenly startled by a very loud noise, which triggered an involuntary reaction much like PTSD. Before I could cope with the first incident, another incident occurred in rapid succession. By that time, I was completely unnerved and was verbally attacked by a total stranger, in what I felt was an unprovoked attack. Needless to say, I was not my spiritual self; I was without reservation or filter, my human self.

In the aftermath of this incident, I was very disappointed in my reaction; I felt like a hypocrite. A hypocrite, by definition is: a person who acts in contradiction to his or her stated beliefs. If you have read much of what I write, you know that I frequently include scriptural quotes and I try to convey the importance of loving others, kindness, compassion, etc.

After much soul searching, I realized the lesson this episode was meant to teach me was this: no matter how spiritual you become, you will always retain some of your human qualities. Only when you have transcended this dimension will the last vestiges of human reaction leave you.

Do I really believe myself to be a hypocrite? Absolutely not, I believe what I present to others to the very core of my soul and I do my best to live what I believe, every day of my life. None of us is capable of perfection in our human form. Romans 3:23 says: "for all have sinned and fall short of the glory of God." I believe a sin is just a human mistake; and as we all come into this world with free will, we will surely make many mistakes. It is how we learn from our mistakes that promotes spiritual growth and that growth is what we take with us to another world, at the end of our human life. We learn very little if we believe we are incapable of making mistakes. I learned a valuable lesson from this very distressing incident. There are two parts to the lesson I learned, the first; that I can't control my every reaction, I can only try to control my actions. The second: that in order to love others, I must love myself enough to readily forgive myself when I feel like I have failed. If I would be gracious to others, I must show the same gracious spirit to myself.

Politeness, or courtesy, was something that was highly regarded in the old school. I learned there is never an excuse for rudeness. One of the issues with that statement is that there are differing opinions as to what constitutes rude behavior in the world, we are now living in. In the old school, failure to say "Please" and "Thank You" was considered rude. It is possible to say nothing and be considered rude. Selfishness when publicly displayed, used to be considered rudeness. When you are rude it is not possible to be gracious; nor can you be gracious and unkind in the same moment. Graciousness is a more lofty virtue than

most; when you observe it in anyone, it is similar to seeing a beautiful rainbow or sunset. It creates an unexpected moment of joy.

21

Compassion

🍎🍎🍎🍎🍎🍎🍎🍎🍎🍎🍎🍎🍎🍎🍎🍎🍎🍎🍎🍎

*I*s compassion a virtue or a value? There seems to be some debate about this question; a virtue is generally considered to be an inherent quality. You either have it or you don't. If this is true it would likely mean it isn't something that can be taught or learned. If it's a value, the opposite would likely be true. My spiritual journey has taught me that we are able to change many things about ourselves, if we have the intention to do so. Nothing about us that isn't physical (eye color, height etc.) is set in stone; we have the power within ourselves to change how we think, what we feel, how we act and what we believe. So I believe it is possible to "become" compassionate.

Compassion is defined as "to suffer together". The qualities compassion induces in us are: patience, kindness, warmth, and a desire to help others. To be compassionate is to be a good listener; someone who listens with patience and genuine concern for the distress of another. It is to be kind and willing to offer your help in order to alleviate the pain of another, be that physical, emotional or spiritual pain. We are often fearful of taking part in the suffering of others, so we avoid those situations that would make it necessary to do so. Spiritual growth requires us to become compassionate, because it is an integral element of love. It is easy for most of us to offer compassion, warmth, kindness, etc. to those we feel affection for, our family and friends. Spiritually, we are called upon to offer these things to all. It is often difficult for humans to see that all are part of "The One". In Matthew 25: 40-45 Jesus said: *Verily, I say unto you, inasmuch as you have done unto the least of these of my brethren, you have done it to me.* "He was talking about showing compassion to all."

We all have our strengths and weaknesses of character. As hard as we try, we will never be perfect as human beings, but you can struggle to be the best possible person and if you lack compassion, you can't reach beyond the level of human being in your journey here on earth.

I believe compassion is an essential part of what we come here to learn. If the world were to become inhabited with more truly compassionate beings, it would change so many things; hatred, anger, jealousy, greed and violence would begin to recede; unity and harmony would take their place.

In the old school, we received a grade for sharing, for being kind, for playing well with others etc.

When I became a mother, I taught those same values to my children, as did nearly everyone else I knew. My children and their spouses have taught them to my grandchildren. I am puzzled as to where the disconnect with such principles took place. Today, as I look around, I see so many instances of children bullying and ostracizing their classmates, of young adults who are focused only on success and greed, parents who seem to encourage only aggression and selfishness in their children. How did this happen?

I am not trying to promote the false notion that none of these things ever occurred in the past, only that they were aberrant behaviors that were not acceptable in any setting. It seems today they often go completely unnoticed, because they have become normalized. However this occurred, it too can be changed, but first we have to recognize it as a problem. It begins with each of us;

we can't change other people, except by example. We can change ourselves though, but only if we truly have the desire to do so.

22

Selflessness

🍎🍎🍎🍎🍎🍎🍎🍎🍎🍎🍎🍎🍎🍎🍎🍎🍎

It is often difficult for children to recognize the value of a concept like selflessness. As children, our sense of self is likely most important to us; we are quite cognizant of our personal, physical, as well as emotional needs.

I was an emotional child; I wanted my thoughts and feelings to be respected and I was very sensitive to the fact that they often were not. I was willing to treat other people with the same consideration, but if they had treated me badly, it became a real internal struggle for me. I never forgot it if someone hurt me emotionally; I would store it away in my mind and heart. I became wary of any future interactions with those people; I tried not to treat them badly, I just avoided them whenever possible.

When I was in high school, I helped host a birthday party for a young relative; she was about 8 yrs. old. She was an extremely emotional person, even at that young age; she still is to this day.

Each time we played a game at the party, she insisted on being first and reminded everyone that it was her birthday, so she was the "guest of honor". Not only did she want to be first, she would quite reluctantly allow someone else a turn and then she wanted it to be her turn again; this was in spite of the fact that none of the other guests had taken their turn. When we refused to allow that, she threw a huge tantrum and held her breath. We were familiar with that tactic and didn't respond in the way she wanted us to; it was a very ugly and embarrassing scene. She wound herself up into full blown hysteria. Today, she is 60 yrs. old and still behaves the same way. She has driven away everyone who ever tried to befriend her, as well as her family. The point I'm trying to make is that selfishness; the exact opposite of selflessness, hurts us as well as those around us.

One of the ways I learned selflessness as a child, had to do with the fact that I always had a strong reaction to some-one else's tears or embarrassment. I was so vividly aware of the discomfort those things caused me, that I internalized their pain. Because of that, I was almost always willing to step aside or give in to them because their pain was hurtful to me, as well. It was really not that important to me to be "first" at anything, as long as I was included in whatever was going on.

In the society we currently live in, selflessness is way down on the list of desirable traits. It can't hope to be noticed in a world where aggressive self-aggrandizement reigns supreme. Everyone seems to want to be the center of attention, all of the time. Instead of being a mark of good manners, it is considered almost cowardly to give way or step back, in order to let someone else step into the spotlight. Our society breeds competitiveness, and being successful shares a direct correlation with being first.

In the old school, such behavior was considered shocking and shameful. Today, if you recognize or comment on the bad behavior, you are the one found guilty of "shaming" others. As a person who was educated in the old school, the world seems completely upside down. In Mark 9:35, Jesus said to his disciples: *"if any man would be first; he shall be the last of all, and servant of all"*. What that means to me is that in desiring to always put yourself first, you place your spirit in bondage.

23

Character

The dictionary defines character as the mental or moral qualities distinctive to an individual. We are not born with our character; it is something that develops over time and many things contribute to its formulation. It is an internal code that governs our actions the majority of the time. On rare occasions people may behave in a manner that is contrary to their character.

At no time is it impossible to amend our character; it isn't set in stone and can be altered upon our wish to do so. In my case, as with many others, my character was formed through interactions with my parents, siblings, friends, teachers, church and community. When I was a child there were some very well-defined expectations set for you by others. I always wanted to please people and I didn't like being in trouble, so I tried to meet these expectations. I didn't always succeed, but I think that could be said of anyone. In today's world, the expectations are not so clearly defined. While I sometimes disliked the limiting nature of the expectations placed on me by other people, I believe they made it easier to navigate life. For me personally, I believe trying to meet these high expectations, caused me to create some very high expectations of myself and I was doomed to failure many times. I haven't always met my own expectations and when I failed to do that, I could be pretty hard on myself. At one point in my life, I considered myself to be such a failure, that I just must not be the person I had always believed myself to be.

I began to act in ways that were totally out of character and the farther away I got from my true self, the more miserable and confused I became. I didn't understand at the time this was happening, that I was seriously depressed.

As I look back on that time now, I see that God used many people to help me find myself again. I don't believe God creates these situations, but I certainly do believe He uses the messes we create, to teach us things of value. What I learned from my mistakes at that time was that if the circumstances are right, you can surprise even yourself and behave in ways that are totally foreign to your authentic self. The authentic self is what each of us needs to find; we need to come to know ourselves through it and allow ourselves to be guided by it.

I also learned not to judge other people harshly when they do things that seem to be out of character. I think most of us go through some period of floundering around, before we find our way. As I wrote the previous sentence, I thought of some people I know who still haven't got it figured out; they seem so lost and unhappy. The last thing they need is condemnation; what they do need is guidance. I know some of these people well enough to know that locked deep inside of them is another person; someone not like the person they present to the world. I think life gives us many opportunities to find ourselves, but we don't always recognize them as what they are and let them pass us by. I can see mine so clearly now; back then it wasn't so easy.

If we are fortunate in life, we cross paths with certain people who become our mentors. They seem to be showing us a way forward that perhaps hadn't occurred to us before. They are people we admire and trust and they seem very confident in their own choices and life path. Not all mentors are people who are uniformly looked up to; some of them appear to be even more flawed than those they are here to guide. These people are easy to overlook, but their wisdom may be the most important assistance we will ever receive from another human being. Mentors don't try to get you to be who they are or do what they do, they encourage you to discover who you are. Life is a voyage of discovery and a mentor is like a navigator who helps correct the ships course, but doesn't take the wheel.

"Character is what you are in the dark when nobody is watching. When nobody knows what you do, or even think. That's your truest colors right there!"

- Dwight L. Moody

24

Dignity

Some years ago, Bob Dylan wrote a song that he titled "Dignity"; it asked the question; *"Has anybody seen dignity?"* It seems as if dignity has disappeared from our lives; he could just as easily have asked, *"Has anyone seen humanity or compassion?"* If you pay attention to the news, it seems as if all of these things are absent from our lives today.

As we have struggled to make it through the pandemic that has landed on our doorstep, we see overwhelming examples of selfishness and careless disregard for the safety and well-being of others. While at the same time, there are those whose bravery, compassion and kindness stand as a testament to good old-fashioned heroism; they seem to be in the minority.

I have asked myself, *"Where does such a widespread absence of humanity come from? How have we become such a selfish and unkind nation?"* America was once a proud nation, dedicated to fostering human rights, peace and dignity in the far corners of the world. What can we do to reclaim the ideals we once espoused? There are no easy answers to these questions, but I believe it is time to ask them and try our best to find solutions that will allow every inhabitant of this planet to live with the basic dignity and humane treatment they deserve.

I became a Bob Dylan fan at the age of 14; at that time, early in his career, many people thought he was a modern- day prophet. I'll admit to wondering that same thing from time to time, when I look back at the lyrics of some of his songs and see that what they predicted has come to pass. I was not drawn to him because I thought he had all of the answers; it was because he always seemed to be asking the right questions. He has often reminded us of the responsibility we bare to treat all of the citizens of the world with fairness, respect, and dignity.

Years ago, I took a Certified Nurse Aide course; through it I learned that dignity is the last right of responsibility we owe to those who are actively passing from this world. How sad it is that so many of us never consider the right of dignity, as we go through life interacting with others.

25

Faithfulness

When considering the word faithfulness and what it means, two things automatically come to mind; faithfulness to God and faithfulness to marriage.

Most of us consider faithfulness to be something we demonstrate in a physical way. If we are faithful to God, we go to church regularly and we say our prayers, but it is possible to be faithful to God and never enter a brick and mortar building that is labeled a church. The church is actually the people who ascribe to whatever form of doctrine has been agreed upon; it is not a building. If we exhibit our faith by simply going through the motions of attending church and saying prayers when it seems called for; do we really exhibit faithfulness? Faithfulness without true love is only superficial and has little value.

In being faithful to our marriage partner we do not have sexual relations with other people; this is a deliberately simple explanation of what faithfulness is. These things, while being obvious because they can be seen outwardly, are perhaps only the result of faithfulness and not the thing itself. Faithfulness is a virtue that has it's being internally. It is this inward virtue that fuels commitment, loyalty and duty, but it hinges on love and devotion.

It is possible to be outwardly faithful to your spouse, because you do not believe in cheating, but not be

72

doing it for the right reason; because you love them and are devoted to their happiness, as well as your own.

In either of these relationships, loyalty without love doesn't feed the union what is necessary for its growth; a deepening of the bond. It isn't possible to be truly faithful without loving that to which you apply your duty and loyalty, as well as, honesty, truthfulness, honor and respect.

For most of us, the easiest bonds of love and faithfulness occur within our familial or blood relationships, but again, this is not always so. There are those instances where a parent rejects their own child or the child doesn't bond with the natural parent. These abnormal situations cause incredible pain to the one rejected and leave the one who turns away from the love that is offered with a feeling of emptiness that can rarely be filled.

Faithfulness in friendship can be a difficult thing because these are frequently relationships built on proximity or common interest, or common lifestyle. They often work for a while and then something changes, perhaps one of the friends moves to another state and the difficulty of spending time together makes the friendship unworkable. Many times, there is no dramatic end to these relationships, they just gradually fade away. The bonds of affection may live on, though the connection is altered.

Our enduring faithfulness to others is a gift we give to ourselves as well. The breaking of such bonds can cause discomfort, at the least, and at worst may cause a deep sense of loss and pain.

Our bond of faithfulness with God will never be broken on His part, only by ourselves can it be rendered inactive.

As with most values or virtues I was taught, there was no class at the old school with the name "Faithfulness" on the door, nor was there a classroom with the label "Integrity". You learned these things in many places and in many situations; often the strongest impressions were made by observing what happened due to a lack of virtue in a real life situation, that occurred as a course of living life.

26

Duty

The definition of the word duty is: a moral or legal obligation; a responsibility. We often think of people in uniform when we think of duty, police officers who's sworn duty is to enforce the laws of our country, state, or city. It is also their sworn duty to protect the citizens of this country and to preserve their guaranteed rights; that's a really important part of what they do. There is no provision in the law that excludes anyone from those protections based on race or ethnicity, religious affiliation, gender, etc. Every citizen of our country has the right to be presumed innocent until found guilty in a court of law, merely being accused of a crime is not enough to legally cause them to forfeit these protections. This includes those we like and those we don't. It includes those who are suspected of violent and heinous crimes. It includes those who are impoverished and living on the streets as well as those who are celebrated and wealthy. It includes both the educated and the uneducated among us. Each of us is entitled to "justice for all". It isn't the duty of police officers to mete out justice, their duty is specific; "to serve and protect" to the best of their ability. It is not to attack suspected offenders who have been subdued or surrendered voluntarily.

We have a duty also; to abide by the laws as they are written, to support the police in the legal performance of their duties and to come to their aide when they are injured or incapacitated in the line of duty. They are not the enemy; they are our family members, friends, and neighbors. They are not the job they hold, anymore than any of the rest of us are what we do to make our living.

It is the duty of the justice system to deal with rogue officers in the same way they would any other offender; according to the evidence presented in the case against them. Even when justice doesn't satisfy our desire for account-ability, as we see it, it is our duty as citizens to seek legal remediation; rioting, burning and smashing is never a legal remedy and often hurts innocent people. Committing more crimes isn't the answer to what you may view as injustice.

The other place we frequently look to when thinking of duty, is the military. A strong military is a deterrent to those who would seek to harm us as a nation. This is only so, if the allegiance of those who serve in our armed forces is to the sitting government, whether it be of either party. The only possible exception is if they receive an illegal order to attack the government or citizens of this country.

We as citizens have many duties also, regardless of whether we wear a uniform; we have duties to our fami-lies, our friends, our employers, our communities, and on up the line to the duties of being a citizen of the world we live in. Sometimes, doing your duty means setting aside your own personal views, including your political ideology, for the sake of the greatest good. We have seen in recent years, the fragility of the democracy that grants us our freedoms.

Few of us grew up in this country, not having recited the "Pledge of Allegiance" many times. It is our duty to protect our democracy every bit as much as those who put on the uniforms of our military forces. The lack of a uniform makes us no less responsible for the health, happiness and freedom of the people of the United States of America. We must hold ourselves to the same standards we expect of those who wear the police uniform or the uniform of any branch of our Armed Forces. Duty isn't something you can put on or take off as it suits your purpose; once sworn it should be a lifetime commitment. If we are not taught to be true to these standards, as we were in the old school, they begin to weaken as we have seen in recent years; living without them creates a precarious environment for all of us. We do not enjoy our freedoms because we are entitled to them; they are a gift given to us by our ancestors, many of whom bled and died to give them to us. Without consistent recognition of their value, they can be taken from us. The constitution of this nation has served us for nearly two and a half centuries, with very few amendments to its original wording. How fortunate we were to be given a document of such relevant longevity; I'm not sure that could ever happen again; just my own opinion.

27

Tolerance

🍎🍎🍎🍎🍎🍎🍎🍎🍎🍎🍎🍎🍎🍎🍎🍎🍎🍎🍎🍎

I grew up in a neighborhood that had about 40 kids, on average. It was very racially diverse; there were Caucasians, Latinos, and African Americans. To us they were all just our neighbors and friends; we knew nothing of racial intolerance until we entered public school. We were shocked to discover not everyone saw our neighborhood friends in the same light we did.

I've always believed that early exposure to people of different ethnicities, helped us grow up without the biases many of our "other" friends exhibited. It was important to us to raise our own children without racial or ethnic biases. I think it is critically important for all children to be given the opportunity to form bonds with others who may look different, or speak differently etc., without distinctions they absorb from the adults around them. As human beings we don't make friends with everyone we meet, but if we look at each individual person with no preconceived ideas about them, there is less likelihood we will dislike or dismiss them without allowing ourselves the opportunity to form a bond of friendship.

There are many kinds of intolerance in the world and it is almost without exception a negative force; it is hurtful. Somehow many children grow up to believe it is acceptable, even desirable to humiliate, ridicule and torment those they choose to target among their classmates. Nearly every school claims to have a zero tolerance policy regarding bullying between students. Yet we see more suicides in children at shockingly early ages, due to bullying by their peers. To be fair, not all or even the majority of bullying takes place in the classroom; much of it happens in hallways, restrooms, lunch rooms, and before or after school hours. Because of the prevalence of social media use by younger and younger children, many are targeted in their own homes; sometimes in the middle of the night. The home that should be a safe haven for them, can no longer protect them from the insidious negativity that intolerance breeds.

How are our children growing up to be so cruel to each other? There are many things you could point to; the fact is, there are so many aspects of society today that foster this kind of behavior. It has become so accepted, that it often goes unnoticed as it poisons the minds and hearts of our children. When tragedy occurs and precious lives are lost, almost no one wants to take a hard look at these influences and place the blame where it truly lies. It's considered "politically incorrect" to blame anyone or anything these days. It's just so much easier to say "well, these things just happen sometimes". We will never be able to stop this senseless loss of life, if we can't be adult enough and tough enough to take an honest look at what is driving this epidemic of destruction. These children are mimicking what they see in adults and even if they don't see it in their own homes, they are exposed to it everywhere they go. They can be targeted by the damage done to their peers, by the avalanche of negative behavior they are allowed to experience vicariously through all types of unrestricted media, or perhaps through violence within their own homes. Children can't live, breathe, be fed a steady diet of violence and intolerance, and then grow up to be kind and caring human beings.

In the old school, the one that included what we were taught at home, at church and everywhere else we went, we were taught to be kind, considerate, polite, helpful, generous, etc. All of these things relate to respect, we were taught to respect the feelings of other people; there was a universal expectation that you would do that. It didn't always happen, but there were repercussions to be faced in nearly every instance when it did not.

The world is a tough place, it can be a cruel place and we are often shocked at the atrocities human beings perpetrate on each other. This isn't the kind of thing that will change direction on its own. It's never easy to turn something this big and this far out of control, but you can't solve any problem until you accept that it IS a problem. I don't envy parents today; it was hard enough to raise children to be decent human beings when I raised mine. Even those who try to raise their children to be kind, respectful and tolerant, must send them out into a world where such qualities are rare and seldom supported.

The only way I see that we can change this trajectory is to teach tolerance in every way and every place we can. As parents and grandparents, we must raise our awareness and focus of what our children see and hear; we owe them a better world, a kinder, more tolerant world to grow up in.

There are many manifestations of intolerance and it isn't only children who exhibit this behavior. Adults in general are often intolerant of the decisions others make for themselves. We do a very poor job of accepting differences regarding such things as religion or spiritual philosophy, political views, gender identification and many other areas of personal preference.

Intolerance is based on fear and most people never examine what lies beneath it. Most people couldn't tell you what they fear or where this fear comes from. They only know something inside is causing them to react negatively to a certain thing; so in essence, they are striking out blindly. If you were to ask them why they find some of these things so annoying that they choose to behave in a such a negative and often destructive way, many would say *"that's just the way I am"*. We give little thought to the idea that we can choose to change how we feel or that others can change how they feel and who they are. We don't allow for growth; we don't stop growing when we become adults. We are constantly changing in every aspect of our lives; but sometimes we choose to stunt our own growth, by being fearful and intolerant.

28

Cordiality

Now there's an old- fashioned word; cordiality, it means "friendly or warm and sincere". There are many people who stand out in my mind as being warm and friendly. They are the first to step out of a crowd and welcome someone new. I was never one of those people.

I was a person who was usually just trying to blend in, or fade into the background, so as not to be noticed. My husband tells me frequently that he prefers to be "front and center". I always prefer the back row; usually in a corner. I always stand back and let someone else be the first to speak up. I have often mentioned that I lived with an inferiority complex for many years and I think my hesitation comes from that. It is still a bit of a conscious effort for me to step up and stand out, but I am much better at it than I used to be.

I grew up living in fear that my parents were going to make us move to another town while I was still in school; I didn't ever find myself in the position of being the "new kid". Thankfully, it never happened to me, but I was always anxious for the kids that found themselves in that situation.

I lived in the same town for over 60 yrs.; it was my comfort zone. I wasn't "friends" with everyone who lived there, but I had at least a passing acquaintance with most of them.

I knew what to expect from them and they, in turn, had a certain expectation of who and how I was and how I would behave towards them. I always speak or nod to anyone who looks directly at me as they approach; it seems rude not to.

There was a certain woman who lived in our town, who I considered to be "unfriendly or not cordial". She worked in one of the local businesses and on occasion I would have to have a conversation with her, in her professional capacity; in that regard, she seemed pleasant and friendly. If I passed her on the street the next day, I would speak to her and she would walk right past me without any acknowledgment. After this happened a few times, I became annoyed with her rudeness and decided not to speak to her again unless she spoke first. What I should have done was to continue to be friendly, even if she never acknowledged it. My bad attitude was just making me rude also. I have no idea why she refused to speak to me, but I doubt it was an effort to be deliberately rude.

I have learned that it is very important for my own spirit to feel that I have treated people well. I haven't always done so, and to the degree that I am able, I have apologized for my actions. It is much more important for me to maintain the peace of my spirit than to behave in a way that is contrary to what I know is right. I don't place myself in a lot of social situations these days, but when I do I make a much greater effort to be cordial; it costs you nothing to be so, and you may be rewarded with a friendly hello or a sunny smile.

29

Community

I grew up in a very small town, it was often referred to as the "community of Peabody". In my mind, the word town refers to the location, community refers to the people living there. The root of the word community is commune, and it basically means 2 things. The first is: a group of people living together and sharing possessions and responsibilities. The second is: to be in a close accord or communication with someone or something.

As life has changed and people move around a lot more, it is difficult for many to develop a sense of community. When I was growing up, you could ask anyone you met, *"Where are you from?"* or *"What is your hometown?"* and the answer came almost instantly and without much thought. If you've had a place that you referred to as your hometown, you will likely wonder why I think any of this is important enough to mention. People who moved from place to place and never established roots, used to be called drifters and were often received with great suspicion, especially in small towns.

A community is more than just a group of people who live in the same place for an extended period of time; much more than the "collective". A community is an entity that is created by the interactive involvement of those within it. They are in many ways like-minded, but not always so. They try to live in accordance with the laws or code of conduct that has been established over years of living together. They are family, friends and acquaintances and most times, have the best interest of everyone in the community in mind. Often, it is hard to see the community in everyday living, because there are disagreements between neighbors, instances of grumbling among those who don't agree with the decisions of the governing body, there is gossip and there are sometimes hard feelings. As long as there are human beings living in communities, there will always be some discord, but let there come a natural disaster, a flood or fire or tornado and you will see the "community" magically appear before your eyes. When help is needed community never fails to show up. Let me give you just one example of this: there was a man who lived across the intersection from us in the town we still call home, though we no longer live there. Most people thought of him as a grumbler, he was always unhappy with someone or something and he was very vocal about whatever it was that displeased him. My husband was a member of the city council for many years and at one point served as the mayor. This neighbor thought nothing of coming across the street to berate my husband about one thing or another when he saw him outside mowing the lawn etc. The city council ran high on his list of dislikes and he frequently made derogatory comments about my husband in public places, such as the local café. After a time, he refused to speak to me if I met him on the street or in a local business. I just considered him disagreeable and left him to himself. This situation existed for a number of years.

Then one day, I was cleaning the blinds in the front parlor of our home and I noticed the man frantically running around outside his home, it was obvious that something was wrong. Then I noticed other people who seemed to be frantically looking for something or someone. I went outside and asked the neighbor what was going on and he told me his two-year-old granddaughter was missing. I immediately joined the search. The child was found about 30 minutes later, safe and unharmed. When he came to tell me she had been found, the relief and emotional exhaustion showed on his face and I felt sorry he had experienced such a scare. He continued to be grumbly and disagreeable, but I had witnessed his softer side and it made his grumbling easier to tolerate. This is what a sense of community can do for interpersonal relationships.

A community doesn't have to be a place where you were born, or even the place you grew up in. It can be anyplace you live if you make a conscious effort to know your neighbors and care about people living around you. Sometimes, community develops by osmosis, simply from living in proximity to someone for a period of time. No matter how it develops, it can add a dimension to your life that is well worth striving for. This sense of community was highly valued in the old school.

Communes or communities as they came to be called, came into being in years past, because it was safer to live in "town", than to be out away from other people. There have always been obligations attached to living in a community, in exchange for the safety they afforded. When you fulfill those obligations with a sense of affection attached, you are receiving something of value, rather than giving because you are obligated to do so

My hometown.

30

Family

❧❧❧❧❧❧❧❧❧❧❧❧❧❧❧❧❧❧❧❧❧❧

*I*t took me about 25 yrs. to really grasp the importance of family. Before that, I thought family was like a group of roommates, they live together, share the same space, and sometimes find each other annoying. In reality, a family is much more complicated than that. It's like a world within a world, a kind of microcosm It has its own structure, usually determined by the parent (or parents). It is like a military chain of command. The greatest authority and responsibility rests with the parents, followed by the oldest sibling to a lesser degree, and then in descending order down to the youngest child. This was the typical family structure during my childhood and adolescent years. I'm not sure there is a typical family structure today, many children grow up with little or no family structure. When my youngest son, Ethan, graduated from high school, he was one of only four kids in his class that had the same set of parents they started kindergarten with. That would seem to suggest that there aren't a lot of typical family situations in our present time. A lack of structure, especially family structure can have a major impact in a person's life.

As human beings, we often resist structure of any kind, but it holds a place of great importance. It frees us to learn the more important things we've all come here to learn. My husband is a

87

person who prefers to live with a lot of structure, he usually provides it for himself. During the years he worked (he's now retired), his ability to create structure earned him a position of leadership and trust, in a job that provided well for our family. I provided the structure in our home life and that gave him an atmosphere in which his non-working life was as calm and relaxed as it could be, while raising a family. Tom creates structure for himself so he can use it like stepping stones. For instance, he can do the mundane things on "autopilot"; that frees up his mind and time to focus on problem solving. By autopilot, I mean things like always leaving for work at the same time, taking the same route every day etc.

Families are made up of individuals with varied personalities, strengths and weaknesses, who are tied together through relationship. Sometimes, the relationship is a blood tie, but often it's out of necessity or choice. Any way a family is formed, the relationships can be difficult, and they are meant to teach us many things that can't be learned elsewhere. It took years of not living in a house with my birth family, to understand the value of those relationships and the valuable training experience it provided, as I moved on to other relationships.

In a much larger sense, we are all part of the "family of man", or the family of God. No matter what name we choose to know our supreme being by, it is the same energy we are referring to. We are God's children, even if we choose not to acknowledge it in any way. We have all come into this world from the same Source and we will all return to the same place when we leave here; beyond that I can't say what happens.

We have much to learn about each other and ourselves. Just as a small family unit should find a way to coexist in love and peace, our greater human family is supposed to do the same. Looking around today, it seems we are farther apart than ever, but it isn't the "bigger picture" that our human eyes discern and it is there we can find our hope for peace and harmony.

This world was intended to be full of trials; it's the way we learn and the way by which we are perfected. It takes a lot of heat and pressure to create diamonds and spirits in human form respond in the same way to adversity. We are made better by the fires we walk through in life, no matter how painful the journey.

31

Volunteerism

●●●●●●●●●●●●●●●●●●●●●●●●

For most of my life, I've suffered from what I call "big sister syndrome", a sense of being responsible for my younger siblings. I learned very early in life to help my mother take care of our family. Many times, in Sunday school, our lesson touched on the importance of helping others, as Jesus had done.

In the old school we received a favorable notation on our report card, if our teacher deemed us to be "helpful". I always tried to help our elderly neighbors when they needed help reaching something in the back of the bottom cabinet, or help threading a needle, or help finding their eyeglasses, etc.

My parents were not the kind of people who volunteered to help the community, but they would help their neighbors whenever they could. My paternal grandparents helped many needy families as part of their Christian ministry. They would provide food or clothing or a temporary place to stay for those who came to ask them.

When I was old enough, I joined the Girl Scouts. The Girl Scout promise reads:

> On my honor, I will try
> To serve God and my country,
> To help people at all times,
> And to live by the Girl Scout Law.

The Girl Scout Law reads: I will do my best to be honest and fair, friendly and helpful, considerate and caring, courageous and strong, and responsible for what I say and do, and to respect myself and others, respect authority, use resources wisely, make the world a better place, and be a sister to every other Girl Scout.

With the demise of many former organizations whose members swore such oaths, promises like these are seldom made and if they are, they are usually ignored as time moves on.

In nearly every area of my life, I was taught to help, to serve, to volunteer. Volunteerism used to be considered a by-product of patriotism. Many people use the excuse that they are too busy, I don't deny it; I see it all around me, people meeting themselves coming and going. For many, life is just a blur; but we all have choices to make. There is no law that says we must continue to live this way. You can opt out of a lot of things that don't serve you; you only do them to meet someone else's expectation.

One of the most famous inauguration speeches ever given was that of John F. Kennedy in 1961. It was a call to service and it inspired a generation of younger Americans to give their time and energy to public service and volunteerism. There are many ways to serve others that don't involve joining things or going to endless meetings. You are never too young to help someone and probably never too old, because even a kind word or a smile is of benefit. If nothing else, you can pray that the help that is needed will come. Anything you do for someone that lifts their spirit and warms their heart is service and it causes a ripple of energy that moves outward and has impact in many ways you will never be aware of.

The Bible teaches us to serve others with a cheerful heart, not for money or to draw attention to ourselves.

32

Patriotism

When I went to kindergarten at the old school, one of the first things we learned was the "Pledge of Allegiance". We began each school day by reciting it. The pledge was originally written by Francis Bellamy in 1892. It was not formally adopted by Congress until 1942. The wording of the pledge has changed slightly over the years; it originally did not contain the words "under God". President Dwight D. Eisenhower asked Congress to have them adopted into the official version in 1954. His reasoning pertained to the fight against communism, during the "cold war".

The pledge was written in a way that included "all"; there were no exceptions written into it, so all means anyone and everyone. It does not exclude any race, nationality, gender, age, etc. It does not favor any one of the "united" states over another; nor does it exclude any form of religion. It does not call our allegiance to any individual person or party.

There are many today, who would have those excluded from not only our official statement of loyalty to our country, but also from the Constitution and the Bill of Rights, who do not look "American", or worship in the "American Way". They would seek to exclude immigrants based on their ethnicity and religion.

There is a quote on the base of the Statue of Liberty in

New York harbor which reads: *"Give me your tired, your poor, your huddled masses yearning to breathe free, the wretched refuse of your teeming shore. Send these, the homeless, tempest tossed to me, I lift my lamp beside the golden door."* The patriotism of the old school was inclusive and compassionate; it didn't question the validity of the need the huddled masses presented when they arrived at our shore, or our borders.

The flag we stood before as we recited the "The Pledge" every morning, has been commandeered by a new version of patriotism and a perverted sense of entitlement, by those who choose to ignore the history of our country.

Forgive my soapbox speech, but I am unapologetically an idealist and I believe we should always try to live up to the ideals we claim represent us. It is those ideals that brought us to this place in time. I'm not foolish enough to think it's easy or even possible to always live up to the highest ideals we set before ourselves; I simply believe we should try.

33

Life Skills

♥♥♥♥♥♥♥♥♥♥♥♥♥♥♥♥♥♥♥♥♥♥♥♥♥

When my older two children reached middle school age (then called Jr. High school), a new class became part of the curriculum; it was called Life Skills. It was a course in very practical knowledge such as, how to write a check and balance a checking account etc. I thought it would be beneficial to teach things that everyone just assumed kids would know or figure out on their own, when the need to know them became evident. I was a bit disappointed that the class didn't address the very fundamental subject of human interactions. This type of knowledge used to be taught at home, mainly by mothers, because they were usually the one at home with their children.

We no longer live that way and the question has become, who will teach these valuable tools needed to navigate the complexities of a lifetime of interactions with other human beings? Unfortunately, in so many instances the answer is "no one." The result of that is the disintegration of the fabric of our society; I'm not blaming mothers for this; I'm only saying it needs to be done by someone. The past few years have shown us to be a nation of irresponsible, selfish, unkind, hateful and violent people, who are only focused on ourselves and our personal success. Success itself, has been redefined to mean "having anything and everything I want, without regard for the rights of others, or for the law of the land, or for the damage done to others."

Even our ancient ancestors had a code of conduct that considered the safety and well-being of everyone within their group. Even life lived in a cave required a certain degree of acceptance of the rules of conduct that were agreed upon by all and were meant to keep everyone safe, warm and fed.

How little we seem to have progressed in our consideration of the welfare of our human brothers and sisters. We seem to have lost our life skills somewhere along the way.

The sad fact is that those who have never known life except as it is lived today, don't miss a kinder and more supportive way of living. Along with the loss of our life skills comes the loss of our dignity, honor and respect as a nation. We are no longer the example we once were of humanity, inclusion and fairness to the rest of the world. We are no longer looked upon with envy by those seeking a better life; one of freedom, safety, and lack of want. We are a great country to whom much has been given and from that we have developed an overactive sense of entitlement and a serious lack of appreciation. Deep in my heart, I grieve, because I know we can be better than this; I know it because I have seen a better life and I mourn its loss.

34

Teaching

If I'm being honest, and I try to be, I never liked school; that said, it doesn't mean I don't like learning. We never stop learning, even when we don't want to learn. Life is teaching us something in every moment, in every interaction. Just as we are all learning throughout our lives; we are also teaching.

We teach others who we are and how we want to be treated. We teach our children in many ways; perhaps the most impactful of those ways is by our actions. Most of us teach our children in more direct ways also; hands on, so to speak. We teach them to walk and talk and how to feed themselves etc. If we fail to love and care for our children, we teach others that we are irresponsible and not suited to raising other human beings.

We teach our spouse that we are loving and trustworthy by whether or not we are faithful to our marriage vows. We teach our spouses that we love them in the way we interact with them and with the children we share with them.

We teach our parents that they taught us well, when we live by the values, they instilled in us as children and when we in turn, care for our parents as they grow older and can't take care of themselves. In doing so, we teach them that they are loved and valued by us to the end of their lives.

We teach our friends and acquaintances that they matter to us and that we are compassionate when we share their pain and grief as they mourn their own losses. We teach them that we care when we are willing to sit and let them tell us their deepest secrets; when we listen quietly and without judgement.

In the same way we teach things of value by our words and our actions, we teach undesirable behavior also. We are constantly being observed by others, either in our own homes or out in the world somewhere, and our actions provide a learning experience for those who observe them. That experience is either positive or negative, and we always have a choice in the impression we leave.

My mother always told us that the way we behaved in public places, reflected on our parents and the way they were raising us. Something about that has always seemed unfair to me. I can understand it as long as children live under their parent's roof, but there comes a time when you alone are responsible for your actions. That doesn't mean your actions no longer impact the lives of your parents and other family members, it just means they are no longer responsible for what you choose to do.

I once knew a young child who was being raised by parents who were unhappy being together, unstable and alcoholic. He was often the whipping post for their unhappiness; he grew up filled with anger, hatred and bitterness. He has spent a great deal of his life in prison; I often have thought that in fairness, his parents should stand beside him when he faces the judge and hears his sentence and that they too should share the punishment he receives. That sentence belongs to them too, though it doesn't work that way under the law, but perhaps it should.

Recently, there was another school shooting, perpetrated by a teenage boy, whose parents gifted him with a semi-automatic pistol for Christmas. Within days, he took it to school and killed several students and wounded others. During the course of the investigation into this tragedy, it was discovered on the parent's social media posts, that they had ignored his unhappiness and threatening comments about hurting people at the school he attended; they are now charged as accessories in the deaths of the students who lost their lives, because of the irresponsibility of their actions.

As I continue to look back at my own life, I have a great deal of sympathy and respect for all those who tried to teach me things I deemed uninteresting or unimportant. I've learned it's incredibly hard to see someone throw away their natural ability to learn and thrive, because they just don't care or realize the importance of what is being presented to them. Teaching requires lots of patience and often, the results desired do not become apparent immediately; that doesn't mean that no learning took root. Some of the wisest words in scripture are found in Proverbs: 22-6 *"Train up a child in the way he should go, and when he is old, he will not depart from it."* The scripture says nothing about the time between childhood and old age, and many people stray pretty far from what they were taught as children. What you are doing when you responsibly teach your children, is laying a firm foundation; your words, that you thought were dismissed, somehow rise to the surface in times of crisis and confusion and light a path for them to return to as adults.

Part 2

Words To Live By

Introduction

$\mathcal{B}$y now, I'm sure you realize that the old school wasn't just a building; it was home, church, family, neighbors, friends and acquaintances. The old school was people! Mr. Rogers, of PBS fame, used to sing a song called, *"Who Are The People In Your Neighborhood?"* All of the people you come into contact with have something to teach you; your job is to figure out what that is. Sometimes, they offer words of wisdom, sometimes they teach by example; for instance, we had the same postman all the years we lived at home with our parents, and when I married, he was still delivering the mail, long after my kids were in school. His name was LeRoy and he delivered our mail to the box on our porch by 3pm nearly every day, except on Sundays. It never varied more than a few minutes; the lessons he taught were punctuality and reliability.

In our little town, we usually had one police officer; sometimes it was the same man for decades; even though they proceeded our time, we knew their names and we considered them to be famous people. Stubb Derby, Bill Reed, Charlie Marsh etc. My own uncle Bernald was the Chief of Police at Belle Plaine, Kansas for more years than I can remember. This handwritten Code of Ethics was posted in his office up to the time of his retirement. There are many lessons we could take from it. All of these officers taught us to respect the law and the rights of others and to follow the rules.

Not everyone whose life intersects with yours will have a positive impact, but the lessons we learn from them are still important; they can teach us what not to do. Life is a balance of positive and negative interactions; it often gets out of balance and we have to use what we've been taught in order to restore that balance.

That brings me to the first old school proverb I want to share. I grew up hearing "old sayings" from many of the people I interacted with; these old sayings are often referred to as proverbs, or old adages, or words of wisdom; they are little statements of bigger truths. When children are young, we often use rhymes or songs to teach them basic things, such as counting

One, two, buckle my shoe
Three, four, shut the door
Five, six, pick up sticks
Seven, eight, shut the gate
Nine, ten, do it again.

It is easier to learn something that rhymes or something put in a song. It is also easy to learn from repetition. The proverbs I learned in the old school have stayed with me all these years, when a lot of other information flew out the window. Part 2 of this book is an effort to share some of those words of wisdom that still hold true today, or at least they should. Many things change over time and no longer apply to your life; truth is always true.

Code of Ethics

As a law enforcement officer, my fundamental duty is to serve mankind; to safeguard lives & property; to protect the innocent against deception, the weak against oppression or intimidation, & the peaceful against violence or disorder, & to respect the constitutional rights of all men to liberty, equality & justice.

I will keep my private life unsullied as an example to all; maintain courageous calm in the face of danger, scorn, or ridicule; develop self restraint & be constantly mindful of the welfare of others. Honest in thought & deed in both my personal & official life. I will be exemplary in obeying the laws of the land & the regulations of my department. Whatever I see or hear of a confidential nature or that is confided to me in my official capacity will be kept ever secret unless revelation is necessary in the performance of duty.

I will never act officiously, or permit personal feelings, prejudices, animosities or friendships to influence my decisions. With no compromise for crime & with relentless prosecution of criminals. I will enforce the law courteously & appropriately without fear or favor, malice or ill will. Never employing unnecessary force or violence & never accepting gratuities.

I recognize the badge of my office as a symbol of public faith & I accept it as a public trust... I will constantly strive to achieve these objectives & ideals dedicating myself before God to my chosen profession — law enforcement.

Linda Burrows   Gerald Burrows

Code of Ethics that hung in the office of my uncle, the Chief of Police of Belle Plaine, Kansas for 24 years.

1

You Reap What You Sow

The two most important words in this phrase are both action verbs: to reap is to harvest (or gather), to sow is to plant. Practically speaking, if you sow wheat, you won't gather a harvest of corn. There's an old song about love that illustrates this concept well; its title is *"You Can't Grow Peaches on a Cherry Tree"*.

There's another old saying that goes: *"You are what you eat"*. If you take that a bit farther you can say, "you are what you think". If you think only sad thoughts, you won't be happy. If you fill your life with angry thoughts, you won't be gentle, or kind or generous. You can't be full of love and hate at the same time; they are mutually exclusive emotions. If you interact with other people with loving intentions; they most often will respond positively. What you are giving will be returned to you, whether it be love or hate, friendship or animosity, conflict or peace. This is a universal law and you can use it to your advantage. In many spiritual philosophies it is believed that we manifest our own truth. Isn't that just another way of saying *"You reap what you sow"*?

Instead of holding on to the concept that life happens to us; we can live our lives believing we are creating the life we want to live, through our thoughts and actions. I do believe there is a plan

105

for our lives that we are party to creating before we come to this world, but it is a general plan and does not impact our freewill to make many of the decisions that determine our life's path.

We, as humans/spirits are capable of manifesting great change in ourselves and in changing ourselves, we change the universe. There is also an old saying, *"Life is what you make it"*, and there is so much truth and wisdom in this thought. Many of these old sayings are full of wisdom. The fact that it is wisdom that originated in times past, makes it no less wise or applicable today. Wisdom and truth are usually very simplistic in nature, but are seldom recognized in their natural form; we seem to think that unless something is complicated, it isn't valid. In learning to recognize truth and wisdom we can calm the chaos within us and the calmer we become inside, the calmer the world outside will seem.

2

Pretty is as Pretty Does

🍎🍎🍎🍎🍎🍎🍎🍎🍎🍎🍎🍎🍎🍎🍎🍎🍎🍎

For nearly as long as anyone can remember, our society has been fixated on physical beauty. It took a huge leap for the worst about the time everyone bought a TV for their home and life began to revolve around what they saw on it. Advertising, in particular, presented only the most *"appealing"* human specimens to sell everything from toasters to roadsters. Less attractive people need not apply.

In Hollywood it was much the same, except for the occasional "character" actor or actress; someone had to play the villain or the old maid aunt. I've often wondered what it must do for you self-esteem to know you've only been considered for a part because of your lack of beauty. Elizabeth Taylor was once considered to be one of the most beautiful women in the world, but she was quoted as saying: *"Beauty really means nothing, if you put all of yourself into the way you look, you are doomed to be disappointed, because looks fade and you have to live with whatever is left."* That's a paraphrasing of her exact words, but you get the idea.

In Hollywood today, there are numerous once beautiful women who fell victim to the desperation of maintaining their youthful looks and succumbed to plastic surgery and botox etc. How sad when people believe they are only as valuable as they are beautiful.

107

The world places so much focus on how people look and little on how they are. We are often deceived by a beautiful face or a handsome appearance. We are deceived because we equate goodness with attractiveness. There is another old saying: *"Beauty is only skin deep."* Our fascination with appearance is symbolic of a deeper problem. We often don't want to look deeper into ourselves or others, because we fear being disappointed by what is lacking there. A pretty or handsome face can hide a lot of darkness, or even worse it can hide an empty soul.

Beauty should be an element of who you are, not all that you are. There are two kinds of beauty: one is a result of your genetic code and is only superficial; the other comes from the innermost regions of your heart and soul. This kind of beauty doesn't fade with the aging of your human body.

Yet another old adage says: *"Beauty is in the eye of the beholder."* We don't all see beauty in the same way; some of us see a beautiful face and some of us see a beautiful spirit. Beauty can be defined in many ways, for instance, the most unattractive woman holding her newborn child is a beautiful sight. A beautiful little girl who throws temper tantrums and swears like a sailor, isn't pretty for long.

I really don't believe we get points in heaven for a beautiful face, after all, what did we do to create it? The answer is, nothing. I do believe we get a lot of credit for the beautiful soul we create. My point with all of this is to observe that we should take more than a fleeting glance at attractiveness and look deeper before we pronounce one person beautiful and another not so much. If we were to do so, we would find beauty is not such a rarity as we thought it was.

3

Roses Are Red

🍎🍎🍎🍎🍎🍎🍎🍎🍎🍎🍎🍎🍎🍎🍎🍎🍎🍎

Roses are red,
Violets are blue,
Sugar is sweet,
and so are you.

My mother taught me many things; sometimes she was angry and yelling at me when she was trying to teach these things and a lot of it didn't seem to stick. My father taught me fewer things, but he rarely ever raised his voice and his teaching moments were quieter and I responded with giving what he said some serious thought. These days I apologize to my mother often; I learned when I had my own children that mothering is often a thankless job.

One of the things my father used to tell me was: *"little girls should look sweet, be sweet and smell sweet; and big girls should too!"* The idea of girls being taught to be sweet is repellent to some elements of our society these days, but as with most things we would be wise not to throw the baby out with the bath water.

If you read what Daddy had to say again, you'll see that it doesn't say "act" sweet, it says "be" sweet. Acting sweet is just that; an act. It's disingenuous, false or insincere. When Daddy said *"be sweet"*, he was fostering a way of behaving; in other words, he meant "strive to be all that is entailed with having a sweet demeanor. Don't be rude or insulting, don't hurt people with your actions or your words, be accommodating and pleasant.

109

That word "accommodating" will likely ruffle some feathers, because many people today believe little girls should be taught to be aggressive, demanding and outspoken in their pursuit of success. To be considered sweet by most women today, would be seen as dismissive.

I would suggest that the "ideal" woman can be successful without being brash, aggressive or grasping. She should be well-informed, well-prepared, well-groomed, professionally dressed (whatever her profession), well-spoken, attentive, a creative thinker, a team player, considerate in her thoughts and actions, measured in her judgements, grateful for the opportunities and support she receives, kind, and yes; being sweet won't hurt either.

4

Everything That Glitters is Not Gold

If you knew me well, you'd know that I'm excessively attracted to things that shine; I LOVE bling. I love jewelry that sparkles when the light catches it just right. I developed my love of jewelry at a very early age; my father smoked cigars when I was about three or four and he always gave me the ring from the cigar wrapper. I wore it around like it was a diamond.

I have rarely been seen without earrings since I was about twelve years old; I've told all of my family, not to forget my earrings when the time comes to bury me. I have also worn glasses nearly all of my life; I don't like wearing them, but if I think of them as another piece of jewelry, I feel a lot better about it. My glasses always have some sparkle too!

I'm one of those people who nearly always sets off the metal detector at the airport. Usually, there is some bling on the clothes I wear or the purse I'm carrying. I think my reason for liking things that sparkle, shimmer and shine, is that I'm always looking for the light.

I keep a 3ft. artificial Christmas tree in one corner of my TV room year- round. It has white lights and the decorations on it change with the season or whatever holiday is approaching; today it is an Easter tree, when Easter passes, it will become a miniature teacup tree until fall, when it becomes a Halloween tree. It brightens the room and lifts my spirits; sunshine does the same thing, but on the days the sun isn't shining, I still have some comforting lights.

There is nothing wrong with seeking light; in fact, it's what were supposed to be doing. God is Light (illumination) and in seeking illumination we focus on the brighter, more uplifting things in life. Where we place our greatest focus, we create the life we live; life does not just happen to us haphazardly, we play a large part in determining the direction it will take.

The point of this old saying is: as human beings we are naturally attracted to bright, shiny objects, but not all things that shine are what they seem. It may be wise to examine them more closely before reaching for them. We all know there is a huge difference in an object made of pure gold and one that is cheap metal that is only coated with gold on the surface. People can be like that also, many times the flashiest, most noticeable people are something else entirely beneath the surface, but you can't see that for the glitter and shine.

We live in a society where so many people seem desperate to get attention, and they will do almost anything to get the attention they crave. They look everywhere to find that thing that will make them feel special, exceptional or valuable, but this kind of value can't be found in objects; shiny or otherwise. What they seek so desperately, is a reflection of something they lack inside themselves. It is self-worth, self-esteem; it is love for themselves, exactly as they are, without adornments or objects. They feel something is missing because they do not feel whole.

What is lacking is only love; they do not realize their limitless worth. We are all whole and valuable and shining with the light of God's love. There is a not so old saying: *"God made you and God doesn't make junk!"* It becomes easier to see the real value of people and things, when you begin to live your life more mindfully, when you live with awareness of the deeper meaning that lies beneath the surface of everyday life.

This is my teacup tree, the tree changes with
the seasons and holidays.

5

An Ounce of Prevention

🍎🍎🍎🍎🍎🍎🍎🍎🍎🍎🍎🍎🍎🍎🍎🍎🍎🍎🍎🍎🍎🍎

We have grown used to the idea of trying to prevent illnesses, accidents, and even death; I would agree that to the extent this is possible, it is a good thought. We all know intellectually that sometimes no matter how far medicine advances, or how much safer our modes of transportation become, or how careful we are with the health of our bodies, things happen that are beyond our control. People become ill and cannot be cured, people do not survive car or airplane accidents etc., and people continue to age out of this world. Living in this world is inherently dangerous; that is a fact we don't like to think about, much less have to accept.

We are conditioned to believe there is a pill or a procedure to fix any illness or injury we might incur. Much of this conditioning happens with the help of various forms of media, such as; television advertising of the latest available drugs, which they now instruct you to ask your doctor if you need. Shouldn't your doctor be telling you what you need? Medical dramas seldom lose a patient, regardless of the degree of trauma the situation presents. Many people have become positively obsessive in their pursuit of health through extreme exercise habits, yet they still die when their time comes. Doctors and insurance companies push us to have so called "preventative" tests done on a routine basis, many of which are designed to detect cancer. To be precise, they don't prevent anything; they can "detect" but they can't prevent what your body is already exhibiting. We are always told that early detection is the key to survival, but once detected, they may wait weeks or even months before treatment begins. They may offer additional treatments even after they have admitted there is nothing further, they can do. Why do they do such a thing; because we are desperate for time, as much time as we can squeeze out of our earthly existence. Perhaps, if more of us truly believed that life doesn't end when our physical body stops functioning, we wouldn't fall victim to such desperation, nor to the false hope further treatment promises.

My aim here isn't to discourage anyone from seeking medical treatment or protecting their health; it's up to you to determine what treatment is right for you. There are many things you can protect yourself from, if you are aware of the danger they present; for example, if you never jump out of a plane at thousands of feet above the ground, there's a very good chance you won't be injured or die in a skydiving accident. If you avoid all bodies of water and only take showers, there's a very good chance you won't drown. Realistically, there are only so many risks you can reasonably avoid and at some point, no matter how carefully you live, your physical life will cease.

Prevention, like so many other things in life, comes down to, choice and focus. You are at liberty to do whatever you choose, and even when you understand the risks involved, you may still be willing to act. It is also important to note that you can't "live" your life being afraid of everything that might possibly hurt you. I think there is another old saying that fits here: *"All things in moderation"*. A little caution and a little consideration will likely get you through most of life's bumps and bruises.

6

Don't Throw the Baby Out With the Bath Water

Somewhere in the back of your mind you may be think-ing; what does all of this stuff about living in the past have to do with living in the world today? Isn't all of this irrelevant to the lives we live now? Every generation, all the way back to the beginning of time, wants to effect change; they want to leave their own stamp on the world. There's nothing wrong with wanting to make things better, but when we change things for the sake of change and lose the meaningfulness of what has come before, or when we lose the wisdom of the ages, we lose so much that is valuable. History is not segments or eras or decades, etc.; it is one long unbroken thread. It has always been and will always be so; until the end of time.

Several old sayings come to mind as I write this chapter; The first is: *"for everything you gain, something is lost."* When a new generation steps up to take the reins and they reject all of the good and beneficial things that have come before, they run the risk of losing more than they will have gained, when it comes time to turn it all over to the generation that steps in behind them. Another old saying that fits here is: *"Don't waste time reinventing the wheel."* That means it often isn't necessary to scrap something someone else put their efforts into creating; in doing so you are taking a

116

step backwards and your progressive agenda may suffer for it.

The old adage that serves as the title for this chapter means this: discard what is without value, but be discerning enough to hold onto what is helpful and meaningful. I know a woman whose mother passed several years ago and it became necessary for her and her siblings to go through her mother's things and decide what to keep and what to discard. When all of the sorting and throwing out was done, it was discovered that sadly, her mother's beautiful wedding gown had been discarded and could not be retrieved. It was a heart wrenching loss that occurred because the person who discarded it was unaware of its value.

In discarding the wisdom of the ages; you are negating the experience and knowledge gained through the every day living and learning of generations of human beings. A treasure trove of invaluable knowledge that in many instances was painfully and painstakingly gleaned.

Wisdom is a cake that takes a very long time to bake; its value is inestimable. Knowledge is built on the steps of each generation's experience. Though we do not all walk the same path; we are all on the way to the same destination.

7

You Can Lead a Horse to Water

There are times in life, when despite our best efforts, we have to admit defeat. No matter how hard you try to help someone, they will always have the choice to reject what you say or what you're offering. Even though it seems crazy, or silly, or ungrateful of them, they can still make that choice. Most of the time, we don't understand such foolish choices; we can't see the world through their eyes, even if we know and love them well. I have often wondered if it's possible to really know anyone as well as we think we do. Human behavior has been studied for centuries and it still puzzles even the experts.

What seems to us to be the only obvious choice, may fail to win some people over to our way of thinking. They have their reasons, of course, sometimes their reasoning may be faulty, but it won't stop them or turn them from the path they are determined to walk; even if that path leads to their destruction. We can never truly know what motivates these seemingly flawed decisions.

We are capable of changing many things, but it is hugely important for us to realize that we can't change other people. That isn't our job; our job is to love and support them the best way we can and sometimes that is the hardest thing to do. When things reach a point where our natural inclination to help

118

them, becomes only enabling them to repeat the same mistakes, we have to ask ourselves if we're doing the right thing
for them. What is the most loving thing to do? At this point, the
right thing may be the hardest thing. You can only hope they
will understand your motivations and frequently, they won't.

Many families deal with these tough decisions regarding someone they love, especially if drugs or mental illness is a part of the
equation. It becomes a heartbreaking scenario and one we should
not stand in judgement of unless we have walked in their shoes

Don't Burn Your Bridges

y husband and I used to like to dance. We had a group of friends who wanted to learn country line dancing; we even took a few formal lessons. Though it probably doesn't qualify as line dance, one of the things we learned was the country two-step. I only bring this up because it helps to illustrate the point of this chapter. In the two-step, you or your partner take two steps forward and one step back. The dancers can suddenly reverse the direction of the entire circle, by switching to the other partner moving forward or backward.

I find that life is like that a lot. Things can settle into a pretty smooth routine, with everything moving in a certain direction and then something shifts you into backward motion. So, considering the fact that there are so many ups and downs in every life, it seems wise to prepare for those times when life throws you a curveball and you suffer a setback. It's not likely you can anticipate when or how you'll be thrown this wicked, deceiving pitch, but you can at least be aware that it could be coming your way. Knowing this brings me to my point, if you know you might have to take a step backwards in order to maintain your balance, it stands to reason that you'd want to know there's some solid ground behind you. There are times in life when we want to move forward so badly, that we don't bother to neatly tie up the loose ends in the situation we are moving on from. This might be a business relationship, a personal relationship or even something as mundane as a rental agreement, that you turn your back on and walk away from.

I think the things we regret most in life are the things we know we could have done better; things left undone, unsaid, or unresolved. When we do this, we often tell ourselves we're leaving it in the past and it can't hurt us in the future. However, sometimes the unresolved past refuses to remain where we left it, and suddenly, there it is, complicating our new situation.

While I'll agree that life is sometimes just messy and there's very little that can be done to clean it up, if you begin to see a pattern of unfinished business or unresolved problems trailing along behind you, it might be wise to take an unbiased look at your past behaviors to determine it you are at fault. Perhaps, this is due to your having walked out leaving unfinished business behind you that demands to be put to rights. You may have assumed it would never be necessary for you to retrace your steps and face the messiness you were responsible for creating, but there it is.

All of us at one time or another, will have to swallow our pride and ask for help from others, and we may also have to listen to the I told you so, that we know will be coming and that we likely deserve. If we have treated these people well in the past, it is much more likely they will be willing to give us the help we need. If we left a previous relationship, not having met all of our obligations that we agreed to be responsible for, it isn't likely they will be willing to place themselves in a position to be compromised again. The failing on your part, not only causes them to be wary of reconnecting with you, it makes them hesitate to trust others who might potentially behave as you did.

The last part of this axiom about burning bridges is: *"you never know when you might have to run back across."* If we give some considered thought to our interactions with people and try to pass on from them in a respectful way, we have nothing to reproach ourselves with, in regard to our association with them.

In a spiritual sense, I believe a connection you make with another spirit is a connection for eternity. You'll be seeing them again, probably many times and in the next life sequence, the tables may be turned and you will be the recipient of their unjust treatment. It is always to our advantage to treat everyone we encounter in life, as well as we can.

9

It's Better to Have Loved and Lost

Giving your heart, or even a portion of it to another, has always been and will always be, a gamble. When we love someone, we become vulnerable, we risk being hurt in a way no physical pain can measure up to. It matters not whether you give your heart, your love, to a friend, a lover, a husband, a child or a pet; the vulnerability still exists. It is only altered by degree, by depth of love, the strength of the commitment, or the longevity of the relationship. In order to receive love, we must be willing to give love in return. Love is a bonding between two hearts and when the bond is broken the pain is deep and damaging; often, as with the loss of a child, the pain becomes physical as well as emotional.

So, you might ask, if such pain can come from loving, wouldn't it be wiser not to do it to begin with? That seems a logical thought; but it is a loss itself. Because the one who would have received your love, will never know it. You will never know what you could have received had you been willing to risk your heart to discover the treasure love offers.

I know of no one who doesn't want to have friends and though there is less risk to the heart in those relationships, they can also end in betrayal and pain. The gain that is to be found in friendship is that it often forms a bond that lasts a lifetime.

123

Many people form lasting bonds with lovers who never become spouses; these relationships can serve them well for many years, but often, due to a lack of commitment and with no formal promises made, they eventually drift apart. The same can be said for many marriages where there is a lack of love or commitment.

Having come out of a relationship where one feels betrayal, it is often very difficult to offer your heart again. Each relationship is peculiar to itself; people can often behave in a completely different way with a different partner. This may be due to different dynamics within each relationship or it could be due to lessons learned in the prior relationship that can help them to avoid the mistakes of the past.

There are no ideal marriages, but the ideal of marriage is to create a relationship so deep and abiding, that it becomes difficult to see where one person ends and the other begins; thus, the fulfillment of the scripture; *'the two shall become as one".*

In my own life, I have suffered the very real danger of losing a child to illness, as well as the reality of losing a child as a result of the actions of another person. In the despair of these situations, your pain becomes so unbearable, that you can have the thought, only for a split-second: *"If I had never had this child, my heart wouldn't have been broken."* In the next second your heart speaks and it says to you: *"No, having this child in my life is worth any pain I may have to endure. What would my life have been without him?"* In my grief journey I have heard from many sources, including the son whose life was taken: *"In the end there is only love!"*

10

If You Want to Dance You Have to Pay the Piper

This idiom generally serves as a reminder that there are usually consequences or a cost associated with everything you do. The easiest example would follow the idea exactly as it's stated. Say you wanted to hire a band to play at a function you're sponsoring; they expect to be paid. You wanted their services and they wanted to be paid; you danced and they got paid. This idea applies to any number of circumstances in life. Say for instance, you are married and decide to have an extra-marital affair; you're having a good time and then your spouse discovers you are cheating and divorces you. You lose your house, your car, your family and half of your retirement; not to mention the damage to your reputation. You danced (cheated) and the bill or cost of your actions came due (divorce). It's all about choices and consequences. It's warning is that you'd be smart to always consider the possible consequences before you decide on the action. In many cases, you might decide against the action you were considering. Many people seem to habitually ignore this step and jump into whatever it is they desire to do, with no thought of the level of severity of the inevitable consequence. Some people are aware of the possible consequences but decide they won't matter if they don't get caught, and of course, they don't intend to. A wise man once told me: *"Someone is always watching."* I learned the hard way, that is absolutely true!

It generally holds true that the consequence of your actions is comparable to the act itself; a little transgression probably won't cost you everything, but a big transgression is usually a gamble so costly it isn't worth the risk.

Before you decide to play to win, you should think about how much you're willing to lose. Bank robbery is a good example: I've never figured out how the guy with the mask and the gun, who only nets about $700 or so, figures it's a worthwhile gamble, when it costs him 12 years behind bars? That's a whopping gain of less than $60 per year of time spent in prison. That's of course, if nobody tries to take the gun away from him and he's forced to shoot them and they die. If that's a consequence he never considered, it certainly wasn't a well thought out plan. Most criminals don't do much critical analysis before committing their crimes, but they often have plenty of time to think about how they screwed up their life, while sitting in a cell. Sometimes, "dancing" can cost you a lot more than money.

11

Don't Bite the Hand that Feeds You

As I thought about this phrase that I've heard so many times over the years, I decided to look it up and compare my thoughts with the general understanding of its meaning. I looked at a popular website called "Quora"; it apparently means: questions or answers." I've used this site before and my general impression is that it is a platform for intelligent discussion. The answer to my question regarding the title of this chapter, was about what I expected to see, here it is: if someone is providing you with necessities, you shouldn't disrespect them or be ungrateful, or criticize their behavior; lest they feel your disrespect and discontinue the help they have been giving. I considered this to be a serious answer to a serious question.

Here is what was found in the comments below it: *"It means that if you bite the hand that feeds you, the person will be physically hurt and getting a tetanus shot is advised. Consequently, the person that feeds you may have to use his or her other hand to refeed you. If you now bite the other hand, and although another tetanus shot may not be required, if within a reasonable time frame, the person might end up with two hands hurting and unwilling, or God forbid, uninterested in feeding you once again. In the end, you will both be worse, unless you're trying to lose weight. Which may or may not be what you're trying to achieve. There's an exception to this reasoning, which requires a sadist eater and a masochistic feeder, but it's obviously R-rated."*

People such as this are the reason it has become nearly impossible to have a serious, or sensible discussion of any topic. I admit to having a serious dislike of social platforms that allow comments; mainly because it gives people who believe themselves to be clever and hilariously funny an excuse to be rude, insulting and insufferable jerks. In the spiritual sense, I love them all and wish them well, I just don't humanly care for their lack of responsibility or their flippant attitude in general.

A reasonable and rational response to the statement at hand would be, if you're using your brain: biting the hand that feeds you, is not to your advantage. If you are speaking and thinking from your heart, the appropriate response to being fed would be an expression of gratitude.

It seems to me that my generation and those before it, as well as the one immediately following, were taught to think about what they said and did. We were taught about appropriate and inappropriate behavior; we came to know the difference. If we made the choice to behave inappropriately, we knew to expect the consequences of that choice. If you knew you were guilty, you pretty much accepted the punishment you received.

My sister used to work as a paraprofessional at our local elementary school. There was a young girl there who often refused to do whatever work the teacher expected to be done. My sister explained to her that it was her choice to refuse, but if that was what she chose, she would have to face the consequences of her decision. The little girl replied, *"We don't have consequences at my house!"* Apparently, judging from the way people in general, behave these days, there are a lot of households in short supply of consequences.

Consequences exist for a very specific reason; they signal necessary boundaries of behavior. Imagine if there were no consequences for murder; how would any of us be safe? How can we make good decisions when the results of our actions are unknown or unconsidered by us? How can we coexist without reasonable boundaries and consequences for crossing them?

The consequences for biting the hand that feeds you could be that you will go hungry or without whatever necessities the hand was providing. You have a choice to accept the help offered you; you can do so with gratitude and probably receive more, or you can push the hand away in insolence and anger. It really is your own choice, and so is the consequence of the action you choose.

12

You Can't Judge a Book

🍎🍎🍎🍎🍎🍎🍎🍎🍎🍎🍎🍎🍎🍎🍎🍎🍎🍎🍎🍎

This old adage usually referred to someone's physical appearance, but I believe it has a more meaningful application when you are comparing outward appearance with inner reality. It's true that it is a very human thing to judge someone initially by how they look, only to discover later, on further interaction that we have misjudged them.

First impressions are often wrong, because people are so much more than how they appear outwardly. For instance, if you see someone riding a motorcycle, wearing a black leather jacket, having multiple tattoos of skulls and daggers etc., your first impression might be that they are a rebel, a non-conformist, a drinker or a drug user and someone who frequently gets into fights at bars. You could be totally wrong; the biker could be a doctor, a lawyer, a professor or a minister; they could be anyone.

When you are required to sit on a jury in a court of law, you are asked to be fair-minded about the guilt or innocence of the defendant, until you have heard all of the evidence in the case. If the defendant comes into court clean shaven and wearing a suit, your impression is likely to be more favorable than if he comes into court looking scruffy and has a tattoo across his neck that reads "kill". If when you hear him speak, he has a very soft voice and a pleasant demeanor, you may find it difficult to believe him guilty of the crime he is accused of.

It is human nature to form opinions based on our first impressions, but they should be recognized as just a preliminary assessment and therefore subject to change upon further examination. First impressions shouldn't be presented as hard facts.

We most often form our opinions based on what we think, without considering feelings(vibes) that come from our heart instead of our brain. The most accurate reading of another person on first meeting them is most likely to come from our head and our heart combined; this could be compared to the difference between a photo of something and a video of the same thing.

The cover of a book is often the most important aspect, because many people are going to make a snap decision about buying it or reading it based on the impression they get from first glance. If they don't like the imagery or colors used, they may reject it before ever reading the information it imparts regarding the content on the inside.

Our mental constructs often lead us astray; our heart, by itself is often guilty of the same, we like pretty packaging, whether we are talking people or books etc. The heart/mind connection is much less likely to do so; consulting both is like having a built in second opinion. The real truth behind the thought *"you can't judge a book by looking at the cover"*, is that it's only fair to those you are assessing, as well as to yourself, to take the time to look deeper before you form any fixed opinions about them.

13

Birds of a Feather Flock Together

Some of the old aphorisms my mother frequently used drove me crazy. This one in particular, I didn't like. When I, in turn, said it to my own children, they didn't like it either; for the same reason, it seems unfair and judgmental. Another old saying that comes to mind is: *"No one ever said life is fair."* That's because life frequently isn't fair; I'm not sure why we think it should be, it wasn't designed that way.

The point my mother was trying to make is that if you choose to associate yourself with people who behave badly, it appears that you not only support their behavior, but that you likely do what they do.

We lived in a very small town and there were numerous gossips who always had their ear to the ground to pick up a good story; it wasn't always necessary that the story be true, in order for it to spread. My mother was trying to teach me the importance of maintaining a good reputation; that seemed like caring overly much about someone else's opinion.

My mother cared a great deal about what other people thought and it took me many years to discover where her abundance of concern originated. She grew up in the same small town we did and in a situation that, through no fault of her own, was somewhat looked down on. She never forgot that feeling.

It also took many years to accept the fact that people are going to judge you by what they see and hear, even if you feel their conclusions are unwarranted. If you think about being in a situation where you have just been introduced to someone you don't know and have no background to use to assess whether you want to know them better or walk away from them, all you have to base your conclusion on, is what you see and your impressions of what they say and do.

It's necessary for humans to form these kinds of judgments in order to decide some very basic things, such as, *"Is it safe for me to be around this person?"* I don't believe these are the kinds of judgements the Bible speaks against, because there is no condemnation in them. You are only using your basic survival instinct to make a necessary assessment.

When you use your assessment to determine whether you consider yourself better than others in some way, that is a critical judgment and it is hurtful, even if you keep your conclusions to yourself. The idea of comparison in order to rate someone's value is self-centered and unfeeling; it also applies to most humans.

I always wanted to get to know someone for myself before dismissing the idea of having them for a friend. I still think that's the fairest way to treat people, but it does have a downside. Sometimes, it's easier not to form a relationship than it is to get out of one after it's been established. Even so, the unfairness of judging people superficially should outweigh any hesitation based on that consideration.

Getting back to birds who flock together, they do it for some very practical reasons; it offers them some degree of safety and they are usually looking for the same kind of food sources and nesting materials. People often gravitate toward others who share their same needs and desires. It is a well-known fact that we seek those we have things in common with. As I think back on the friend relationships I've had, I see some common characteristics that I am apparently drawn to; most of my best friends have been very out-going, friendly and often outspoken. I have rarely been considered to be any of those things. Perhaps, it's true that opposites attract.

When we are taught the difference between good behavior and bad, the way we recognize it is to observe the behavior of others and compare it with what we believe is right. Is a comparison actually a judgment? I believe that's only so, if the judgment becomes a condemnation. If we are able to observe others and allow for the fact that the differences between them and ourselves are naturally occurring due to situation, culture or environment etc., they are only an observation.

Sometimes we are able to say *"To each his own, or people have a right to be who and how they truly are, or everyone doesn't have to be the same."* It is often best, though sometimes hard, to wish someone well and continue down the path that seems to make the most sense to you. Often, we least relate to those who have something greater to teach us, than to those we are most comfortable with.

14

Nothing Lasts Forever

his statement on first examination, appears to be true, however, a closer look reveals something different. While it is true that in the world of men (the world of time), nothing lasts forever, it is also true that we come into this world as spirit in human form. We do not shed our spirit in order to become human; but we do shed our human body to return to complete existence as spirit. As spirit, we have always existed and will continue to be in existence; spirit cannot die.

It only occurred to me recently, that the world of time is encapsulated within eternity. There is no place where eternity ends and time begins. It exists simultaneously and when our time on earth draws to a close, we simply shed our human body and return to the expansiveness of spiritual existence.

That expansiveness is everywhere; it's not up there or out there, it's just here. The only reason we were told something other than this universal truth, is that many of us struggle to believe what we can't see or haven't experienced. It is easier for us to see and believe things that are more concrete concepts. God is not an old man with a long beard, sitting on a golden throne that's floating on a cloud somewhere; God is being, God is intelligence, God is creation, God is love and God is spirit. Jesus said in John 4:24, *"God is a spirit, and they that worship Him must worship Him in spirit and in truth."*

The Bible tells us we are created in the image and likeness of God; God is spirit and so are we. This is the only way these scriptures have ever made any sense to me. I have heard them all of my life, but it is has only been since my spiritual eyes were opened, that I began to understand. This is my belief that is based on my personal experiences and what I feel has been revealed to me by my spiritual guides.

This doesn't mean that only people who believe as I do will be in heaven, but I think all will eventually come to a place of similar belief. As the hymn "Just As I Am" states: We will all come, just as we are; we do not need to be perfected in the eyes of the world in order to be accepted in heaven. Spirit is forever and ever; it needs no justification to return to it's prior state of being.

15

Don't Shoot Yourself in the Foot

🍎🍎🍎🍎🍎🍎🍎🍎🍎🍎🍎🍎🍎🍎🍎🍎🍎🍎🍎🍎

*Y*ears ago, there was a particular man who served our little town as mayor. Overall, he seemed to do a pretty good job, but his main concern always seemed to be: if something goes wrong, who do we lay the blame on? There's always a chance that something will go wrong; that's just the way life is. It is human nature to want to place blame somewhere when things do go wrong. If you have to decide at whose feet to lay the blame, before you make your first move to remedy whatever problem has arisen, you are severely limiting both your thinking and your actions. You are also stifling your ability to create something of value. Why you might ask? Because you are beginning on a negative footing and negativity doesn't produce positive results.

Most of us find it hard to lay blame at our own feet, even when we were the one who made the decision that was foolish or not well thought out. Often, we choose to do something we know is wrong, but it's something we really want, so we do it despite our own misgivings. The outcome of a decision based on such a thought process is inevitably bad and sometimes it's disastrous. In that case, we look everywhere else to place the blame for our erroneous decision and the havoc it wreaks in our lives.

It seems that many people today aren't interested, or aren't capable of looking to themselves as the cause of their own misfortunes. They blame life, or others, or fate etc. Sometimes, it's a fact that someone else is to blame for something in our life that turned out to be damaging to us; sometimes there is damage to our public image. I've always hated to feel like my misfortunes were fodder for public discussion. I also hate to feel like I've disappointed someone else, but perhaps the hardest thing for me is to accept that I've disappointed myself. This is the reason, I believe, that we so often blame others for our mistakes; it's less damaging to the ego.

Often, we are the ones who need to look deep inside ourselves and admit we are no more perfect or less perfect than others. We are often the cause of our own disappointments, but once we admit it, it doesn't follow that we should beat ourselves up over this admission. Instead, we should accept our responsibility and then focus on making changes that will have a chance of creating a more satisfactory outcome in the future. In other words, we can "stop shooting ourselves in the foot!"

16

Truth Will Out

Being truthful sounds pretty easy, until life becomes more complicated, as it generally does as we become adults and the tendrils of ambition, desire, and relationships become entangled. For children, the truth is much simpler, because their lives usually lack the complexity of that of adults. It can still be difficult for some young children to tell the truth, because at a certain age, they begin to consider the consequences of being truthful. In the mind of a child who is old enough to understand that telling the truth could mean they are going to face an unpleasant consequence, telling a lie may seem like the rational thing to do. They are not sophisticated enough in their thinking to understand that when the lie is discovered, it usually leads to a more severe consequence than the truth would have required.

Most children aren't very good at telling lies; unfortunately, people get better at it as they get older. As a young child, my oldest son, Brett would tell me even before I asked what happened that made his brother cry: *"Mommy, I didn't hit Jeffy with that truck!"*

I remember when I was a child and I didn't make it home when I was supposed to, I would rehearse what I thought was a great story as to why I was late. When I did that, my mother wouldn't even ask me to explain. If I didn't have a story prepared, she always asked me why I was late.

The consequences of telling lies as an adult can be much more severe. In order to hide our bad behavior or neglect to do something we said we'd do; we tell a lie; then we tell more lies to cover the first lie. After a time, life becomes so much more complicated and stressful, as we are forced to continue to lie to try to stay ahead of the lies we have told. It also becomes difficult if we didn't tell everyone the same lie, then we have to try to remember which lie we told to which person. Life can become one gigantic web of lies that we've captured ourself in and depending on the damage we have done to others or to our own life and reputation, it can seem like there's no way out.

No matter how skilled you become at covering your lies, the truth will always find a way to surface. It may take years for it to happen, but a lie will haunt you until its secret is revealed. Living with the fear of being exposed can cause us discomfort that we don't recognize the source of. Lying is really a form of self-sabotage and it's rarely worth it in the end.

17

If You Can't Say Something Nice

Recently, I saw an article in the news about a celebrity chef and former actress, who had been reduced to tears by the unkind remarks of someone who told her on her webpage, that she needed to lose weight. I never cease to be amazed that people feel or believe it is their right to say mean spirited and ugly things that hurt someone.

The creation of online social platforms, chat rooms, etc. seems to have unleashed a virtual tidal wave of insensitivity. As a child, I was taught you can think anything you want to, but if it is hurtful or harmful, keep it to yourself. The world doesn't need you or anyone else constantly dumping your unkindness into the flow.

There is another old saying that comes to mind here: *"Sticks and stones may break my bones, but words will never hurt me."* Unfortunately, that isn't true; words are powerful and they do all manner of harm, especially if they are harsh and cruel. Words can also bring great comfort and support. As with many things, the impact of words depends on the intent with which they are used.

Many people excuse rudeness and insensitivity by claiming they just don't have the same filters others have. Perhaps. That is true in some sense, but that can be circumvented by simply giving some thought to how your words may be received and if you truly aren't meaning to hurt someone, choosing to say something else, or nothing at all. Any of us can change ourselves if we choose to. Unless you really meant to hurt someone, there is no reason that you would not immediately apologize for your unkindness.

Some people think of their unkind words as "constructive criticism"; the only time that's valid is if someone asked for your opinion, because otherwise it's just criticism cloaked in a false pretense. Other people believe they can say whatever they want and then offer a fake apology.

If you don't like apologizing, then you should take greater care to see that your words and actions don't make it necessary for you to do so. I used to have a really hard time admitting when I was in the wrong and thus it was very difficult for me to give voice to an apology, even when I knew I was clearly in the wrong. Thankfully, that has changed since the transformation that's occurred in me, following the passing of my son.

I consider all of this transformation to be miraculous, but the part that involves forgiveness and acceptance of my own imperfections, is a miracle in and of itself. I know, as others can't possibly know, that this change could not have happened without the transformation that began to occur when I was forced to build a new life. That was the impetus for the self-examination and healing that has taken place within myself

We are never too old or too far gone to change, to become better; it is one of the reasons we are here. We are also here to learn to love others as we love ourselves. Sometimes, learning to love yourself is the hardest thing of all.

18

Time Heals All Wounds

🍎🍎🍎🍎🍎🍎🍎🍎🍎🍎🍎🍎🍎🍎🍎🍎🍎🍎

Once in a while, I still hear someone say *"Time heals all wounds."* Of course, this isn't true; time heals some things, but it is often powerless to heal. There are wounds that run so deep, that even the passage of many years or decades can't erase the pain you have had to endure. I am not alone in believing that the loss of a child is a wound that can never be completely healed. This doesn't mean that you can't live a happy and full life, in spite of such a loss. If by chance, there is another loss greater than living in a world without the child you loved so dearly, I question whether I could endure it. Thinking with only my human senses, I can't fathom how anyone endures the loss of multiple family members at the same time; if I think with my spiritual senses, I know that no one ever lives through a tragedy alone, heaven is always there to support you and this fact alone tells me that we can survive the greatest losses life puts in front of us.

When tragedy occurs in your life and you make it through the initial stages of grief; there comes a day when you must begin to rebuild your life. I hesitate to use the word "rebuild", because you can't rebuild exactly what you had with a piece or pieces missing; you must build a new life and this seems like an overwhelming, if not impossible task. It takes time;

143

as long as it takes. No one has the right to tell you how long it should take. They are not walking in your shoes.

Many times, parents find themselves so altered by their loss, that they seem as strangers to each other. The statistics for divorce regarding bereaved parents are staggering; 92% of couples cannot find a way to build a new life together. One of the most common reactions to loss is to withdraw from others, even those you love. We turn inward to try to find safety and balance. Often, people grow apart as they reexamine which parts of their old life will work in the new life they hope will offer them peace and a degree of happiness. In many instances, what is needed most is space and enough time to try to right your personal ship. Trying to determine for someone else how much time is enough time to complete your internal healing, only leads to impatience and frustration. If you truly love someone, you should be willing to give them the time they need.

Having said that, there are situations where no amount of time is going to heal the damage that's been done. I'm only saying, it isn't wise to rush into such important decisions while grief is fresh and the sad fact is, people don't grieve in the same way or at the same speed. It is important to do your best to maintain communication while you are experiencing these strong emotions. Communication is not always verbal; if you know your spouse well, you can read many things from observing their moods and actions in daily life. Many men do not seem able to verbalize their grief, and many women are so overwhelmed by their own, that they find it hard to interact with someone who won't just come out and say what they're feeling. These are not insurmountable problems, if approached with love and patience.

Time is most often more successful at healing physical wounds; wounds of the heart and soul are out of its reach.

19

The Early Bird

here are many things I hate about being late; the fact
that it causes me unneeded stress, is perhaps, at the top
of the list. I already mentioned that tardiness wasn't toler-
ated in the old school and we tried hard to get there on time.
Mornings at our house when I was growing up, were usually
chaotic and many times we ran to our seats just as the last
bell was ringing. When my kids took Band classes, the instruc-
tor instilled in them the thought that *"if you aren't 15 minutes
early, you're late."* In other words, time marches on and we'll be
marching on without you!

We were taught that tardiness is a sign of rudeness, disrespect,
and carelessness. Many times, tardiness is caused by a failure
to plan for the unknown, unforeseen events, such as having to
wait for a train to pass or your car doesn't start. Sometimes, it's
caused by an unrealistic idea of how long it takes to get from
point A to point B. Lateness is not always due to carelessness.

The main point here is that tardiness can cause you a lot of
problems that you might easily avert if you allow more time to
get where you are going. I lived in a household with 4 males;
my husband and three sons. When we all had to be ready to
go somewhere at the same time, all of them could be ready

in about 20 minutes; it takes me from start to finish about 45 minutes. I learned to schedule my time accordingly and they were still usually tapping their feet and yelling *"Mom, let's go!"*

My oldest son is almost paranoid about being late for work; he arrives in the parking lot about an hour before it's time for work. It gives him a chance to have some time to settle in before the busyness of the day.

I like for things to be as calm as possible and being late causes me stress and distress; it disturbs my peace. Maintaining my peace has become much more important since the shock of losing my youngest son; it's a necessity now.

It has become something of a rare occasion for me to attend public events these days, but when I do, it seems that almost no one pays attention to the time the event is scheduled to start. Many people walk in 15- 20 minutes late and disrupt the program or proceedings by allowing the door to slam behind them and noisily talking as they find their seats, etc. It is also seemingly acceptable to walk out in the middle of a performance while talking loudly and slamming the door. There are times when a late arrival can't be helped, but a quieter entrance or exit is something much more able to be controlled.

I understand that we now live in a different world that doesn't have much regard for the old school ways of doing things, but perhaps the world would be a calmer happier place if it did.

A family picture from years ago when we
were busy raising our three sons.
Left: Jeff (5), Right: Brett (7), Front: Ethan (3)

20

You Can't See the Forest For The Trees

Have you ever come close to running through a stop sign because you were looking at the stop light in the distance? Or have you missed seeing a red light at night because there were too many other signs with lights along the same area? These are some examples of not seeing the forest for the trees. There are times when we are so focused on something that we fail to see what is right in front of us that may have more importance.

When my son Jeff began walking at 9months old, he would be so focused on where he wanted to go that he never looked down at what was on the floor in front of him. He walked for about a week and then discovered he could run toward whatever he wanted. He fell over everything that got in his way; things like shoes or toys etc. He fell into every piece of furniture we owned. I finally got rid of my coffee table because he fell into it so many times and I was afraid one of the corners was going to put his eye out. My grandmother, who lived in another state actually thought he had a large birthmark on his forehead because there was a mark in every picture, I sent her. She realized one day that the mark was in a different spot in each picture and that it was actually a bruise.

We are all this way, to some degree; we're always trying to

get somewhere or accomplish something and we "keep our eyes on the prize." It's good to have focus, but how much of life do we miss when we live only to arrive at the journey's end? The journey itself is life. Living life in this way is like only reading the chapter titles of a book. The story is in the pages of text.

I have always had a bad habit of not reading directions before I proceed to do whatever it is I'm working on. I think that may be a result of being left-handed in a right-handed world; most of the time the directions are written for a right-handed person and they don't make a lot of sense to me. Nevertheless, this gets me into trouble sometimes, and undoing what I thought was right that wasn't, is usually harder and more time consuming.

We all look for shortcuts; easier ways to accomplish things or get things done more quickly, but what do we miss by doing so? I think we have become so focused on getting things done quickly, that we have learned to be satisfied with results that are far less than the best we can produce.

In the old school, quality was very important; it wasn't enough to know the answers on your test, if you hurried through it so fast it was unreadable or if you didn't read the directions and the answers were not in the form requested. Teachers in the old school were often heard to say, *"stop ,look and listen!"* That's still good advice and you may be sur-prised at all you've been missing if you decide to give it a try.

21

Never Put off Till Tomorrow

I used to be a great procrastinator. I think I was about 30 yrs. old before I moved past it; though I'll admit there are still times I put off unpleasant tasks as long as possible. Most procrastination is harmless, but occasionally you put off something with the intention of doing it later, or tomorrow or next week and suddenly, it's too late; the opportunity is gone.

In another of my books, I wrote about the experience of putting my Great Aunt Anna in a nursing home. My intention was to visit her at least once a week and the only time I didn't do that was the week she passed away. It had been an exceptionally busy week for me; it was in the back of my mind that I needed to go see her, but I just kept moving it to the next day and then the next. Her death was harder for me to accept because I felt like I had not only let her down, but that I had missed my last opportunity to show her that I cared about her.

There is another old saying that fits into this narrative: *"He who hesitates is lost."* I'm sure I've missed many opportunities because of my hesitation. I have a tendency to overthink things sometimes, which means I often don't act quickly enough. There is a fine line between being fully informed and prepared before jumping into things and thinking them to death. I try to always have good intentions, but the word intention is a noun; it has no action. Unless you put your intentions into action, they serve no useful purpose; they don't move you or anyone else forward.

There is another old saying that fits here as well: *"The road to hell is paved with good intentions."* An intention is only a thought until you put it into action. In many ways it's no more effective than wishing for something to happen. If it's possible for you to turn your wishes into reality, then you should take the necessary action to "make" them into a reality. Not all wishes fall within our ability to create, for instance, if I say "I wish it would rain." I am powerless to make that happen. If a wish fulfilled would cause harm in any way, then it should be disregarded or rethought; it should never be your intention to cause harm either directly or indirectly.

We all say we wish this or that, from time to time, with no intention of making the wish into a reality. It's a lot like thinking out loud. Not all thoughts are required to be acted upon.

Every action begins with a thought or an intention, and I believe every good intention deserves some credit, even when it isn't acted upon. A positive thought impacts the universe in a positive manner, even if it's never shared with another. Our thoughts, just like our actions and our words have tremendous power; we should always use them with care.

22

You Can't Unring a Bell

🍎🍎🍎🍎🍎🍎🍎🍎🍎🍎🍎🍎🍎🍎🍎🍎🍎🍎

As children we were taught that if we hurt another person with our words or our actions, we needed to apologize. An apology can't undo the damage, but if it is sincerely and voluntarily offered, it may help to minimize it.

When I was in Jr. High School (now known as Middle School), I had a close friend who came from a large family; she was one of seven children. If a disagreement occurred between two or more of the siblings, their mother would force an apology and then make them hold hands for a designated period of time. The issue I have with this is that a forced apology is meaningless; professing to be sorry when you aren't serves no purpose. In this case, they said they were sorry to pacify their mother, not to mend a rift between them and their brother or sister. Forced compliance with anything only breeds resentment.

With even a little conscious discernment, it is fairly easy to tell if an apology is sincere. If you are only sorry for your actions because you got caught in the wrong, any apology you offer is only an extension of your bad behavior. They are only empty words and they do nothing for the one you wronged or for yourself.

The concept of regret isn't only meant to resolve awkwardness between two parties, it's also, and perhaps more importantly meant to increase your empathetic sense of the hurt someone else may be experiencing.

As an adult, I had another friend; my relationship with her lasted nearly 40 years. She would often discuss personal decisions she was considering and I would give her my honest opinion about whatever she was thinking she would do. It was a close relationship and she usually took what I said under advisement, even if she was unconvinced and rejected it. Then came a time in her life when she made a decision to create a false narrative about someone in her family; that decision forced everyone around her to publicly support her lie.

She convinced herself that the lie would be the best thing for the person it was created to protect and I don't doubt her motives for doing so. The problem was that we lived in a small town where nearly everyone knew it was a lie. I was one of the people drawn into protecting this falsehood.

I had long since learned that living a lie had a poisonous effect on your life and everyone around you. I wasn't given a choice; I was just expected to support the lie in order to support my friend; a test of loyalty I suppose.

One day, my friend and the person she had created the lie about (who knew nothing about the truth the lie was designed to hide), came into my antique shop and I inadvertently said something contradictory to the false narrative. I didn't even realize my mistake until my friend came back into the store and confronted me. She was beyond furious and I was completely shocked at the way she behaved toward me. I apologized numerous times that day for my inadvertent mistake, and after a "cooling off" period, I sent a card with a complete explanation of how and why it happened; I received nothing back from her, not a card or a phone call etc. There was never any indication that she had accepted my apology.

Shortly after this eruption in our friendship occurred, my son was killed and my life changed completely. She sent a sympathy card with only a signature. I saw her in passing a few times after that and we exchanged polite greetings and nothing more. It has been over seven years since the day she verbally assaulted me and there is an awkwardness between us that apologies won't fix.

When I misspoke that day in my shop, I rang a bell. When she attacked me in her rage, she rang a bell; no amount of time or regret can change what happened. I forgive her for her anger towards me, even though she has never apologized for the way she spoke to me. I am still hurt by it today, even though I've tried hard not to be.

The point of sharing this story is that there are things that happen in life that can't be fixed, no matter how hard you try or how much you wish they could; many of these things involve words.

Proverbs 13:3 reads; *"Whoever guards his mouth preserves his life; he who opens wide his lips comes to ruin."* James 1:19 reads; *"Wherefore my beloved brethren, let every man be swift to hear; slow to speak; slow to wrath."*

23

You Win Some, You Lose Some

The society we live in places winning on the highest pedestal. Losing is unacceptable and losers are dismissed as nonentities. Children learn as young as 3 or 4 years old that winners are celebrated and losers are ignored. Before you get the idea that I am completely against organized sports, let me say; my husband was an athlete in high school and briefly in college, my sons all played various sports as children and through their high school years, one of them played football for a year in college. This isn't about trashing youth sports, but sports play a large roll in our national fixation with winning and winners.

If you've ever "won" at anything, you know the sensation of happiness and pleasure that accompanies it. There's nothing inherently wrong about wanting to experience such feelings over and over again. It only becomes an issue when we allow ourselves to be programmed to believe our worth as a human being is tied to being either a winner or a loser.

Our life experience is about contrast and balance; when there is no contrast, we begin to take the good things for granted or to not recognize the value of doing your best and being proud of that even when you aren't the winner. Life wasn't created for us to always win or feel on top of the world. There will be trials and failures in every person's life and I'm convinced they will learn much more of value in those times, than when they taste victory.

We are not teaching our young people to be gracious winners or to recognize the skill of play of the opponents they have defeated. We make ourselves feel better by having someone to look at as less than.

Trying to create positive feelings for ourselves at someone else's expense creates negativity. God doesn't create negativity, we do it ourselves with our attitudes and actions. When we look at ourselves or at others as either winners or losers. We diminish them and ourselves as human beings. Our true value lies not in winning or losing, but in how we "play the game"; it's in how we have treated others in our time here.

When my children were young and involved in youth sports, my husband Tom was usually their coach. He taught his players to play as a team, to support each other, that the whole team is responsible for a loss as well as a win, and to be gracious whether they won or lost. If they really got hammered, he'd say: *"Well, at least we looked good in our uniforms or don't worry about it we'll get them next time."*

When life becomes all about winning, everyone loses.

One of Tom's baseball teams, Tom is standing in the
back row with the white shirt.

24

Don't Cry Over Spilled Milk

🍎🍎🍎🍎🍎🍎🍎🍎🍎🍎🍎🍎🍎🍎🍎🍎🍎🍎🍎🍎🍎

I spent a lot of time over the years, obsessing about things I couldn't change. What I really needed to change was my own thinking. I've learned that thoughts have power; lots of power. They can help you, or if you let them, they can hurt you; sometimes thoughts actually ruin people's lives.

I think a lot of people get in the habit of seeing only the negativity in life and often don't realize how damaging that is to themselves and to everyone around them. We all get upset or angry about things, but if we realize that in most cases, that is just a waste of our energy (power) and doesn't help anything move in a positive direction.

It isn't always possible to find something positive in every situation, but you'll never see it's there if you aren't looking to find it. We often let some really insignificant thing that goes wrong, ruin our outlook for the entire day. Spilling coffee on the blouse you planned to wear to work, shouldn't have the power to put you in a bad mood for hours; the only way it can do that is to give it that much meaning, it is always a choice we make.

We all have days when nothing seems to go right; but I wonder how much our negative thinking contributes to those situations. If you begin to take mental notes and add up how many irritating things happen in a given period, you will obviously conclude that you're having a bad time.

We don't have to allow negative thoughts to control our mental narrative; we can make an effort to push them away. One of the easiest ways I've found is to replace them with feelings of gratitude for something more important that you recall. It's really impossible to feel negativity and gratitude at the same time.

25

You Can Catch More Flies With Sugar

The full statement is: *"You can catch more flies with sugar than with vinegar"*. As a child I wondered why anyone would want to catch flies to begin with? I could understand catching lightning bugs, they're at least somewhat entertaining; flies are just annoying.

Of course, the point here is that people will more likely respond to you and whatever you are asking of them if you approach them with kindness. If you request something from someone with a sour attitude or in a negative way, the likely response will be, a resounding no, and will reflect the manner in which you asked.

However, the idea that being nice will always get you what you want, is misleading; it only gives you a better chance. It is also necessary that the niceness, you are presenting must be genuine. If it comes across as false-ness, you will be putting yourself in an even worse position.

People these days seem to feel they are entitled to have everything they want and if they demand it, they will receive it. There's another old saying that fits this situation: *"Asking isn't getting!"* Many people just can't accept that *"No"* is a legitimate response to their requests. Instead of asking for something else, or considering the appropriateness of the manner in which they asked, they simply keep asking for the same thing in the same way. As well as being childish behavior, that almost never has a positive outcome.

We spend a lot of time thinking, but we seldom consider that our "way" of thinking might be holding us back from achieving what we strive for. For many people, it comes as a genuine shock to learn they can control their thinking, instead of being controlled by it. The real purpose of this old adage, is to get you to consider your own behavior and how it can sabotage your plans.

26

You Learn More From Your Mistakes

Most of my life, it has been nearly impossible for me to admit my mistakes. It was probably a little bit harder to admit them to myself, than it was to confess my mistakes to others. I don't consider myself to be a perfectionist, but in some areas of life, I do set high standards for myself. Over the years, I have learned not to obsess over every little thing that doesn't meet my self-imposed standards. When I truly began to live by the concept of learning from my mistakes, my life began to change in some very positive ways.

Perhaps, in my case, the biggest changes have been in the area of creativity; allowing myself to rethink something that wasn't working the way I envisioned it, gave more freedom to my thought process. Often, the mistake would force me to think "outside the box" and the finished project would have a higher level of design, than I had originally planned.

In a religious sense, I was taught early in my life that many mistakes are also considered to be "sins". I read a quote a few years ago, that turned that around to the thought that sins are really just mistakes. There was a time in my life when I considered myself to be beyond redemption; I thought my sins were so grievous that God would never forgive me. Then, I realized that it was God who gave me free-will, so He had to have known I would make mistakes; no one on earth can avoid making some mistakes. When I began to understand why I'm here, I realized it was to learn and mistakes teach us so much, so they too are part of the bigger picture. It is part of the totality of human existence to experience failure, as well as success; neither would have meaning without being able to see the contrast between the two.

27

Don't Count Your Chickens

$\mathcal{I}$ think all of us have a tendency to think that certain things are going to happen and that certain other things will not. I have learned that it really isn't safe to assume anything. What you assume is usually what you want to have happen, but it rarely works that way. If you think about assumption in the same way, I believe it makes sense to think about worrying, it becomes obvious that you are wasting time and thought, on something that probably isn't going to occur.

It has taken me many years to realize that the best way to live, is to just let life come to me as it will and not to try to steer it in any direction. This doesn't mean you shouldn't have a plan; it only means you may have to adjust your plan based on what actually happens, that at present is unknown to you.

I have come to believe that things usually happen the way they are supposed to; even when they seem to make no sense and are not at all what we would want.

As parents, we assume when our children are born, that they will outlive us; obviously that isn't always the case. Things happen in our lives that are completely unpredictable, and when they do, our plans for the future are destroyed. We struggle to formulate a new plan, and we must do this at a time when we are deep in grief and may not even want a future that doesn't include the child we have lost.

Since Ethan's passing, I have heard him say many times, "stay in the now!" That means: don't try to live in the past and don't look too far into a future that doesn't yet exist; just deal with the present as it's unfolding.

Jesus said in Matthew 6:34 *"Therefore, do not worry about tomorrow, for tomorrow will worry about itself. Each day has enough trouble of its own."* He didn't mean there will be trouble every day; only that we should not anticipate what the future will bring, before we have experienced the present. If you think about it, it's always now at any given moment. Sometimes, we are so wrapped up in anticipation of what is coming, that we forget to actually experience that present moment in a meaningful way. As our lives pass us by, we remember the significant things, like births and birthdays, accomplishments like graduations or awards, illnesses and deaths. For a moment consider how many moments have passed us by that we are unable to recall at all; can you see the importance of living mindfully so that you create more memorable moments to recall?

28

Tis' More Blessed to Give Than to Receive

🍎🍎🍎🍎🍎🍎🍎🍎🍎🍎🍎🍎🍎🍎🍎🍎🍎

These words of wisdom are actually from scripture, found in Acts 20:35, the words are attributed to Jesus. Similar sentiment can be found in many of the world's ancient religious scripts. Here is a quote from Buddha: *"If you knew what I know about the power of giving, you would not let a single meal pass without sharing it in some way."*

In the Hindu religion, the Bhagavad gita speaks of three types of giving: A gift without expectation that blesses both giver and receiver. A gift given reluctantly and with an expectation that is harmful to giver and receiver. A gift given regardless of the recipient's feelings or at the wrong time is also harmful to giver and receiver.

Why is it more blessed to give than to receive? Because it is a double blessing to give; it blesses you as well as the one who receives your gift. Everything you give, returns to you; it is a Universal law. It does not return in the same physical form, but the energy returns to you magnified from the amount of energy or love you released. The more you give the more you receive. This is not to be confused with the idea that you spend money to make money; this kind of giving must be without expectation of any kind of return. This kind of giving is done with a cheerful heart, without reservation or condition. When you give in this way, the first thing that comes back to you is the warm feeling you get in your heart; a sign to you that giving makes you happy and joyful.

29

Slow and Steady Wins the Race

❦❦❦❦❦❦❦❦❦❦❦❦❦❦❦❦❦❦❦❦❦

At first glance, this old adage would seem to be counter-intuitive; how could you win a race by going slowly? If the race you have in your minds eye is a competition, like on a track, for instance, this saying would apparently make no sense. Even if you were picturing a horse race, going faster as opposed to going slower, seems to be the most important factor in winning. Consider however, that in many instances, if you shoot out of the starting gate too fast and the race is a long one, you are likely to out run your endurance. The race isn't likely to be won by the first horse (or person) out of the gate, but by the one who runs the most intelligent race and is able to cross the finish line first. There are many situations in life that require a similar strat-egy; it's vital in these situations that we "pace" ourselves. It isn't human nature to do that; we want to race as fast as we can toward whatever finish line or goal, stretches before us.

Pacing yourself requires several necessary principles; patience, self-discipline, courage, faith; and mental as well as phys-ical endurance. Winning a race of any kind may hinge more on mental toughness and preparation, than physical endur-ance and speed. Being able to keep to your prescribed pace when you see others passing you by, requires a great deal of mental discipline. Knowing they can pass you and you still have the ability to take the lead in the end, requires faith in yourself and being aware of your own strengths and weaknesses.

Why are human beings so impatient? Because we are governed by time; we hear the clock ticking and we know that time will someday run out for each of us. The more we adhere to the regulation of scheduled time, the faster our lives seem to speed by us. Todays life is regulated by scheduled time; a time to rise each day, a time to leave the house to arrive at work, a time for lunch, a time to leave work, a regular time to retire for the evening, appointments etc. even our vacations have a scheduled time to begin and end. It's hard for us to imagine a world without time.

Humans have not always lived this way; just a few generations ago, we rose when the sun came up and went to bed when the sun went down. People used to say: *"We go to bed with the chickens!"* Even today, that means you go to bed early; when the sun goes down. I find it interesting that a lot of people suffer from what is called seasonal affective disorder; it's related to the shortness or lengthiness of the days. In other words, when the shorter days of fall and winter arrive, some people react adversely to the accompanying reduction in the amount of daylight they are exposed to. They feel a sudden reduction in their energy levels and often experience some depression as well as sleep disturbance. Our human bodies were not designed to live the way we do now.

You might be thinking that even when people rose with the sun and went to bed with the chickens, they had to have a schedule. They did; it just didn't follow the clock in the way ours do now; they knew what they wanted or needed to do on a particular day, they did things in a certain order and they were cognizant of how long the day would be, but they didn't schedule things at 1pm,2pm etc.

Perhaps, you are wondering what relevance this has to life today? While I realize it isn't possible for the majority of us to live today as people did generations ago, I do know from my own experience that we don't have to be a slave to time. There are areas of our lives that we can reclaim, or at least take some breaks from the regimen that the clock sets for us.

There are a lot of little ways to do this; take weekends for example; it is your choice to schedule your kids for all kinds of weekend activities such as basketball, flag football, dance etc. or you can choose to sleep late and enjoy a nice brunch together before attending to your list of chores. You can choose to take a nap while the laundry is sloshing away. You can go for a walk while the dishwasher is running; These are only ideas to help you see that you can control what you put some of your time and focus to. I raised three sons and I haven't forgotten how busy you can be, especially if you also work every day, as most people do these days; I'm simply trying to remind you not to be a slave to time. When you have an opportunity to enjoy some of your time, do so, and do it without feeling guilty that something else needs your attention. There will always be things you just can't get to; learn to accept that and choose wisely what your priorities will be. It doesn't make the world a better place if you feel guilty about not being super human and always on top of things. You will be a much more pleasant person to be around, if you don't feel harassed and harried all of the time. Take a little time to play or just to be, you deserve it and you'll be the winner in the end.

30

Expectations

In writing this book, I have laid out clearly the expectations that existed in another time. Most of the expectations I recalled were those of other people and I have tried to live my life with those expectations in mind. I have often failed to be guided by, or live up to them and when I have failed, they caused me to regret my actions that stood in direct contrast and conflict to them. They were presented to me as a personal system of guidance, a kind of primitive GPS that was designed to help you navigate the often- murky waters of life on planet earth.

This having been said, it is important to think about our own expectations of our behavior and of who we believe ourselves to be. I have read so much about the "authentic self"; perhaps the most important entity entitled to an expectation of you or me. The authentic self should never be confused with the egoic self; the one that fills us with a sense of entitlement and self-importance. The one that encourages us to be selfish and unconcerned with the expectations of others. The one who tells us that others have no right to have expectations of us and that we should turn our backs on those expectations with disregard and disdain.

The authentic self is the one we should expend our greatest efforts to try to reclaim; this is one of the greatest lessons we are here to learn: who are we really? Our human experience helps us grow spiritually; it has no other purpose. The knowledge we gain here contributes to the collective consciousness. Heaven is really just an objective observer of our experiences; they are not seen in the light of good or bad. They are only seen as opportunities for growth and learning.

When your actions cause you to experience the pangs of regret, it is your authentic self that you have truly acted in opposition to. We usually call it conscience. Your authentic self is the one that knows you and loves you to the very core of your being. It knows who you really are and when your actions are not in line with who it knows you to be; it causes you to feel disappointment.

While it is true that we can't live our entire lives trying to please others, it is also true that in order to find real happiness and peace, it is important to know who we really are and to attempt to live our human lives in harmony and balance with that self. It is the spark of divinity that lives within each of us.

Perspective

As I come to the end of my time spent writing this book, I think it's important to look back over what I've considered and included in its pages. Let me begin by saying, that in writing these things, I do not consider myself to be a paragon of virtue, by any means; I am as flawed as any other human being. What could come across to you as "preaching", is merely my attempt at reflection on the way things were when I was a child and my attempt to glean from the teaching of my youth, any valuable wisdom that could be helpful in today's chaotic world. Some things are so purely true, that they are always true and timeless, as well. They do not merely serve as wisdom for a time, but for all time.

Thanks,
J.S. Schmidt

www.ingramcontent.com/pod-product-compliance
Lightning Source LLC
Chambersburg PA
CBHW041952130726
48010CB00029B/381/J